THE WHITE STRIPES

THE WHITE STRIPES

COMPLETE LYRICS
1997-2007

THIRD MAN BOOKS

Copyright © PEPPERMINT STRIPE MUSIC

Third Man Books, LLC
623 7th Ave S
Nashville, TN 37203

A CIP record is on file with the Library of Congress

Art direction by Jordan Williams
Design by Amin Qutteineh
Cover photograph by Patrick Pantano

ISBN (Standard Edition): 979-8-98661-452-6
ISBN (Special Edition): 979-8-98661-455-7

Words and music by Jack White

All rights administered by SONGS OF UNIVERSAL, INC.
All rights reserved used by permission
All lyrics reprinted by permission of Hal Leonard LLC

I Prelude 2

A BAND NAMED DE STIJL
by Hanif Abdurraqib 5

FOREVER THE UNION -OR- I'M FINDING IT EASIER TO BE A GENTLEMAN
by Ben Blackwell 9

STRANGE PILGRIM
by Caroline Randall Williams 17

II The Lyrics 22

THE WHITE STRIPES 25
DE STIJL 57
WHITE BLOOD CELLS 83
ELEPHANT 115
GET BEHIND ME SATAN 145
ICKY THUMP 181
SONGS FROM SINGLES, COMPILATIONS, AND MORE 213

III Rough Drafts & Ephemera 244

The White Stripes

Jack White is a twelve-time Grammy-winning musician, producer, and actor. He is best known for his work in the bands The White Stripes, The Raconteurs, The Dead Weather, and as a solo artist. In 2009, he also founded his own record label, Third Man Records.

Hanif Abdurraqib is a poet, essayist, and cultural critic from Columbus, Ohio. His book *Go Ahead In The Rain: Notes To A Tribe Called Quest* became a New York Times bestseller, was a finalist for the Kirkus Prize, and was longlisted for the National Book Award. His second collection of poems, *A Fortune For Your Disaster*, was released in 2019 by Tin House, and won the 2020 Lenore Marshall Prize. In 2021, he released the book *A Little Devil In America* with Random House, which was a finalist for the National Book Award, the National Book Critics Circle Award, and the The PEN/Diamonstein-Spielvogel Award for the Art of the Essay. The book won the 2022 Andrew Carnegie Medal for Excellence in Nonfiction and the Gordon Burn Prize. Hanif is a graduate of Beechcroft High School.

Ben Blackwell is The White Stripes official historian. Also a co-founder, co-owner of Third Man Records, he's directly overseen the release of over 950 different titles and the pressing of over seven million pieces of vinyl.

Caroline Randall Williams is a multi-genre writer, educator, performance artist in Nashville, Tennessee, where she is a Writer-in-Residence at Vanderbilt University. Host of the Viola Davis produced series *Hungry For Answers*, she is also co-author of the NAACP Image Award-winning cookbook *Soul Food Love*. Her debut poetry collection, *Lucy Negro, Redux*, was published by Third Man Books, and turned into a ballet by Nashville Ballet. The production made its television debut as part of PBS's *Great Performances* series. Named by *Southern Living* as "One of the 50 People changing the South," and ranked by *The Root* as one of the 100 most influential African Americans of 2020, the Cave Canem fellow has been published and featured in multiple journals, essay collections and news outlets, including *The Atlantic*, *Essence*, and the *New York Times*.

I

PRELUDE

A BAND NAMED DE STIJL

by Hanif Abdurraqib

I have all but run out of ways to romanticize becoming one of those musical elder statespeople, shaking my fist at the present while longing for the past. And yet, I want to say here and now that I long for the physical object, always. Something to run my hands over while songs rattle the glass in a window, or send the trunk of a car into a fit of trembles. I came up in the era where cassettes transitioned to CDs, but no one in my house believed the technology would last—plus the tapes got good and cheap once the CDs started filling shelves, and so it was cassettes or nothing in my house. Reading the liner notes of a cassette required *real* labor. A strain on the eyes if the interior notes were robust enough, the small folds of paperwork unraveling like an accordion. But you did it. At least you did it if you were like me, a kid obsessed with language, who liked to read the words in advance, before even pressing play on an album. I liked to imagine how they might sound in the air, the sonic or aesthetic choices that might be attached to them by a rapper, or a singer. I didn't have the language or capacity to understand this concept at the time, but I was very much building a world where language itself was a physical object. Malleable—depending on who was holding it, who was wielding it, who was in charge of how it arrived.

If someone was cool and they thought you could maybe be cool one day, they'd pull you aside after a show sometimes, and hand you a CD. One they burned, some handwriting scrawled haphazardly across the lower crescent. When I was a teenager, going to Midwest punk shows, I was not cool. But there were people who thought I could be cool. One of them handed me the second White Stripes album they'd burned for me. I'd never heard of the band before, and all that was scrawled on the CD was *DE STIJL* neatly—in all caps—and since no words were spoken in the exchange, I was left to assume that the CD I pushed into my car's old player was an album from a band named De Stijl.

The great thing about the burned CD is that as far as physical objects go on the musical front, it is much like language. It can take the shape of whoever is the architect of its delivery. By that, I mean that the version of *De Stijl* that was shoved into my hands (without language), was not burned in order. All of the tracks were there, but it was sequenced in the way that the CD maker most wanted to hear it, or most wanted me to hear it. What this meant for me was the first White Stripes song I ever heard, as an eager teen, was "Little Bird," and the first White Stripes lyrics I heard, weaving in and out of a perpetually bending guitar: *I got a little bird / gonna take her home / put her in a cage / and disconnect the phone.*

I've always been drawn to Jack White's voice, though it isn't necessarily the singing that draws me in, though he can certainly carry a tune in his own signature way. It's more the way words sound coming out of his mouth. When I'm talking to young poets, I do this trick, which doesn't actually make a lot of sense in relies on a kind of absurd minutiae to get its point across. I tell them to not think of the voice as an instrument, but to think of language as the instrument and the voice as the amplifier through which the instrument travels. If nothing else, it prompts writers to be more thoughtful about how language can be a symphony. How it can travel, in tandem with whatever other sonic forces are at play.

My affection for the lyrics of Jack White, renewed in the text here, stem from his ability to create that symphony while also relying on what some might foolishly consider "plain" language, but what I mean, here, is an admiration of a writer who does their best work turning away from met-aphor—which is, in some ways, turning away from softening the harder details of a world, a life, a moment. And in doing so, leaving a listener a wide space with which they can imagine the best and worst of a potential outcome. The merits of understanding the blues, as I've always believed it, was understanding that even the songs about love can be, (should be) a little ominous, slightly wicked, waiting for the other shoe to drop—dis-satisfied with the specific flavor of affection, or at the very least, invested in a haunting. *You've got her in your pocket, and there's no way out now. I'm bringing back ghosts that are no longer there.* It's a series of these moments that feel like someone is tapping you on the shoulder and pointing at something massive, something life-altering that has been in front of you the whole time, you just haven't been hip to it.

I wish I read more people who talked about Jack White as a writer of lyrics, or as a narrator of a very specific kind of interior. He writes in between compelling contradictions—ones that delight me, as both a listener and someone who lives within the contradictions most commonly at play, and who doesn't necessarily view them as contradictions. There are ghosts everywhere in the lyrics, obsession with colors, obsession with exits. Evil and optimism wrestle with each other, longing and a hunger for loneliness tussle in the same bed. Cynicism and desire, rage and tenderness. All of these things seamlessly stitch together and come alive on the page in such tight windows, you barely even notice. Take for example, "I Can't Wait," which is teeming with a kind of relatable bitterness in its first act, our hero cursing a lover for leaving, certain that she'll come back once the world lets her down again. But then, a gentle volta arrives in the songs second act, despite the inferno of repetitive rage in the chorus, and we learn that our speaker is simply afraid of being alone again. Absence is the muse. And sure, someone specific will do to fill that absence, but in the face of real, actual pain, maybe anyone can make it work. These are the kinds of love songs that still speak to me the most. The ones where a writer knows that love isn't guaranteed, but not being loved still has accumulating consequences, and one can only bear so many of those before the scale tilts in the worst direction.

I love this collection of lyrics, mostly because I have always appreciated Jack White—first as a writer, committed to the oral tradition in the same way that elders and pals I've had forever commit to the oral tradition. You tell a story once, and then the story evolves alongside your living, and then someone else gets to tell the stories when you're gone. When I was a teenager, coveting my burned CDs and my shitty car that barely played them, I would scrawl lyrics in a notebook. Ones I loved, ones I wanted other people to see. On the outside, I'd scrawled *In your little room, working on something good.* It's what a girlfriend of mine at the time would shout to me whenever I got into my head, or whenever I zoned out, not wanting too much of the world to filter in.

And so when I say I love a physical object, or when I say I love, plainly, reading words and hearing them in my own head, even when the song isn't playing, I'm also saying that I love the emotional touchstones that language can evoke. I'm also saying that as a writer, I love remembering that as rich and full as a song or a poem can be, even if it is teeming with brilliance and beauty and ache. There is always the simplicity of language on a page. The first doorway. Which, if you're lucky enough, opens up to a brilliantly furnished room, one that feels new every time you step in, no matter how many years have passed.

FOREVER THE UNION -OR- I'M FINDING IT EASIER TO BE A GENTLEMAN

by Ben Blackwell

Jack White and I have had many arguments. In the forty-plus years we've known each other, these disagreements have, more than anything, been about colors. So while the point in the spectrum where red can ever-so-slightly verge into the realm of pink or orange vis a vis printing White Stripes artwork has thankfully never led to us trading blows, it has found either of us exiting a room in a huff on more than one occasion

Jack and I have only once argued about lyrics.

While transcribing the words to "I'm Finding It Harder To Be A Gentleman" for the insert included in *White Blood Cells*, I typed out this line:

If I held the door open for you it wouldn't make your day.

A quick check-in on Jack's end had him correct me:

"It's '*would make your day,*'" he said.

To me, that didn't make any damn sense —

If I held the door open for you it would make your day.

Never mind the fact that the way Jack pronounces the word on the record *sounds* like he's singing "wouldn't."[1] I was more preoccupied with my perception — however specific to my underdeveloped teenage brain it may have been — that my girlfriend's day was not made by me opening doors for her.[2]

---

1 My observation here is joyously buoyed by the fact that proofreaders for this book, when listening to the song unaware of the matter and transcribing with their ears alone wrote out "wouldn't."

2 In hindsight I feel like I was so hell-bent on opening doors…to cars, to buildings,

"No...if you open the door, it makes her day," he countered with all the matter-of-factness of a math teacher expressing the inflexibility of a simple equation.

That did not compute. I explained.

I thought the whole "harder" part of the lyrics meant that there was no acknowledgement, no appreciation, no discernible benefit to actually being a gentleman at the dawn of the twenty-first century.[3] And with that being the case, why would you even bother? Of course the manners you've been taught will slowly die away...there's nothing to reinforce them nor any tangible evolutionary benefit to keeping them alive.

I say this not to unimpressively insert myself into the situation. Rather to illustrate the point that lyrics, whether intended or not, can be so incredibly up for individual interpretation that even their mishearing can feel profound.

And while I hear the collective chorus of everyone reading here sighing "duh" in response to the thought, I still have a particular beef with this construct. The fuzzy area of interpretation still frustrates me. I want it to be clear cut black and white. No pink or red or orange. No disagreement. Straightforward. Unapologetically unable to be misconstrued or recontextualized. It's the reason that I constantly and consistently correct people. Speaking in person. Writing online. Wherever I encounter factual errors or misrepresentations, it bugs the living shit out of me. I get stuck on the dumbest inconsequential reading of the error...*what if in 500 years this is the only recorded mention of the matter...I cannot let it go uncorrected!*

The incongruity of creative artistic interpretation against cold factual

---

2 (cont.) whenever possible, multiple times a day...that the act lost any special meaning and just became viewed as a performative gesture. I wanted more credit than that commensurate with the action of opening a door. I wanted over-effusive praise and astonishment and to be treated like the Second Coming. I wanted the act of opening a door to *make her year*. I thought that ALL I needed to do was open a door. I should've put additional effort in literally any other aspect of being a loving, caring partner. It would be years before I understood this. This was entirely on me. It says nothing about my girlfriend at the time.

3 I'd peg this as the germination of *Elephant* being dedicated to "the death of the sweetheart" as the throughline from gentleman to sweetheart is fairly direct.

truths seems to be a diametrically opposed binary that I've personally struggled to balance in my head for decades. As a collector and a historian and an archivist, I pride myself on factual accuracy. I also consider myself a poet. I write poems. These two concepts feel at odds with each other, not just in general, but as they exist within my being. And they crash together with glorious frustration in Jack White's lyrics.

Around the release of *White Blood Cells,* a conversation materialized amongst a group of folks close to the band. We couldn't help but think that the song "Expecting" was a shot at the band's booking agent, with its "You sent me to Toledo, Toledo, Toledo" lyrics. They'd played a couple shows in Toledo by that point and, well, it's not like anyone would ever willingly *want* to go there. Years later, in a casual conversation with TMR co-founder Ben Swank, he said "I always thought that song was about me." Specifically, how his girlfriend would make *him* go to Toledo while they were both living in Detroit…forever a fifty-four minute fool's errand southbound on I-75…even though *they were both from Toledo.*

Similarly, no less than three people have confided in me that they were the *sole* inspiration for the finger-in-your-chest lyrics in "You Don't Know What Love Is (You Just Do As You're Told)"… a song where the mere relaying of its title caused Bob Dylan to take a sharp intake of breath, as if to say *that's a bit strong.*[4]

Upon the first time really absorbing the lyrics to "Wasting My Time," I asked Jack if the line about idols walking next to him was specifically about Dan Kroha from the Gories. An esteemed local Detroit band that to this day provides much inspiration from their fearless and against-the-grain approach, Dan was one of the first fans and supporters of the White Stripes. At the time it felt unbelievable that he would show up to the Stripes' gigs, let alone become a friend and confidant to both Jack and Meg. Without flourish, Jack's response to my question was, "It's much bigger than that."

And therein is the simple beauty of these lyrics collected here, my frustrating inability to attribute them to something explicit and clear. Tied to the inexplicit hope of anyone who ever writes anything creatively…that

---

4 *MOJO* magazine issue 164, July 2007

any line can seem so micro-targeted to the exact specific scenario that you are currently living through and, at the same time, be bigger than all of it. So it feels foolish to even write it out here...but I have no idea what any of the White Stripes lyrics are about. [5]

I say that from a realm of specificity...clearly there are songs about love or about pain or about childhood...but one thing that elicits fervent respect and frustration from my perspective, is that Jack White has just about never really come out and said "song A is about person B."

To take it even further, a bit of promotional text released with the announcement of the *Get Behind Me Satan* album in 2005 included this chestnut of diversionary embellishment...

Meg: Jack, are these songs about you?
Jack: No Meg, they're about you.
Meg: I wish
Jack: No you don't. You know I don't write about myself or my friends, let alone my sister.

In his faithful commitment to stick to his guns and be broad, throw people off the scent and distract interpretation via commentary about his own lyrics and inspirations, Jack breathes added life into his already vivid and compelling words. That so many people can see themselves within these stories, their lives and relationships paralleled to the narrative on the microphone...well, that's a testament to their strength and to the universality of their reach.

Following my tendency to be thorough and complete in fascination of art and creativity through continuity, my commitment to THE IRREFUTABLE TRUTH has managed to open a can of lyrically entangled worms that has only complicated things, even within the realm of legalities. All just through my own fact-checking for this essay.

---

5 Two exceptions:
1. "Jumble, Jumble." Its lyrics are so basic that Jack explicitly omitted them from the *De Stijl* album art, seemingly out of embarrassment. That one is about Meg falling asleep on a couch. He told me.
2. Jack once introduced "Little Bird" as being about St. Francis of Assisi, patron saint of animals. That tracks.

Fact: the lyrics to "The Union Forever" are made up entirely from lines of dialog cherry-picked from *Citizen Kane*.

Fact: the original mix of "The Union Forever" did not include the 33-second long "there's is a man" a cappella interlude after the second chorus.[6]

Upon receiving a CD-r of the rough mixes from the Stripes first of two stints tracking the album at Easley-McCain Studios in Memphis, I expressly asked Jack why he didn't include that a cappella part, the one he'd sung when performing the song originally with his bands Two-Star Tabernacle and Jack White & The Bricks. His answer was, plainly, "I forgot."

So once back at Easley a few weeks later, Jack recorded the austere vocal interlude paired with the metronomic tapping of Meg's sticks against the rim of her snare drum. This was a different arrangement than done with the previous bands, mainly out of necessity of not having to go and re-record the whole damn thing. But the words proved to be that much more impactful being removed from the music of the previous verses… punctuated by a crashing exclamation point on the word "five" before melting back into the rest of the pre-existing portion of the track. The snippet was seamlessly dropped into the song in the mixing process and no one would be the wiser that "The Union Forever" wasn't actually recorded exactly the way it's heard on the album. I felt *so* proud catching this omission and even more so that it led to involved action from the band. *My attention to detail affected change.*

Initially these "there is a man" lyrics were uncredited on *White Blood Cells* out of ignorance both youthful and blissful. Not until Roger Ebert's *Movie Answer Man* syndicated newspaper column (telling the story of a parent's surprise at their children unexpectedly singing along to the song during a screening of *Citizen Kane*) did it even become widely known in the public consciousness.[7]

From there, lawyers got involved and credits were eventually updated to include one Pepe Guizar, a songwriter from the turn-of-the-century

---

6 This original mix would finally see release on Third Man's 2021 archival release *White Blood Cells XX*

7 Column published February 23rd, 2003

nicknamed "the musical painter of Mexico." To this day, his estate still gets paid 50% on all uses of "The Union Forever."

The problem is, I'm not sure how it even got there. Guizar has only ever been credited as writing the *music*. Originally titled "A Poco No," the song was likely first noticed by *Kane* writer/director/producer Orson Welles via its inclusion in the 1938 film *Noches de Gloria*. There seems to be no doubt or argument that the *words* to the song (specific to the characters and setting of the film) were penned by RKO Radio Pictures in-house lyricist Herman Ruby. These words are the only element present on the song featured in the film that Jack interpolates into "The Union Forever." Guizar's "A Poco No" melody, not to mention his lyrics (which are not featured in *Kane*), are nowhere to be found in White's song.

But no matter how deep I dig...I can't find any instance of Ruby having any proper *credit* for this song. Essentially considered ephemeral in the context of a film from the first half of the 20th century, there's not even consensus on the *title* of the song, colloquially referred to as "Good Old Charlie Kane" or "Oh Mister Kane." Sometimes it's simply listed as "Charlie Kane." Outside of the film itself, I cannot find evidence of the song ever being issued anywhere...never once on a release of the score or soundtrack or a "Music From..." *Citizen Kane.*[8] And in the confusing world of song publishing, there is no extant proof or documentation that this "Kane" song was ever registered to declare Ruby's authorship and rights ascribed to it. Or Guizar's even, for that matter. This all feels important. It feels like it NEEDS to be shared. Facts and truth are necessary.

So It would be foolish for me to not also point out that the opening lyrics to "The Union Forever" ("It can't be love, for there is no true love") are wholesale lifted *from another song featured in "Citizen Kane,"* and no one seems to acknowledge *that* truth.

---

8 The case has been made to me that this whole fiasco around "The Union Forever" may be better off just letting sleeping dogs lie. As there's a verifiable injustice here, attempted to have been corrected once already, it feels disingenuous to ignore. Best case scenario...no one even controls "Oh Mister Kane" and it's an abandoned work free and clear to include and interpolate anywhere without question. Worst case, the wrong party has been paid undue royalties for nearly twenty years and those rightfully due their monies expect to be properly paid regardless...AND maybe someone needs to get credited and paid on "In A Mizz." We have tried, again and again.

In the aftermath of the original revelation in the Ebert column, the initial press reports about "The Union Forever" in 2003 all seemed focused on the cribbing of the song "In A Mizz." Jack spoke about "Mizz" as the impetus to writing "The Union Forever" in an interview with *Rolling Stone* magazine in 2001.[9] Written by Charlie Barnet and Haven Johnson in 1939, "In A Mizz" would see release as a 78 rpm on Bluebird before members of Cee Pee Johnson's band with Alton Redd on vocals were filmed covering the song for inclusion in *Citizen Kane*.

The point to all of this is...even with the best of intentions, with all the prestige and respect and importance conferred upon two songs being featured in (and one with lyrics specifically written for) *the most celebrated film of all time*...intent and authorship and credit are still largely subjective and subjected to the whim of interpretation. All to say that in the end, words written for a pinpointed, precise purpose (while still being poignant and personal), will always have the potential to be rediscovered, reinterpreted and reborn many moons later.

So what happened with "Oh Mister Kane" (and, to an extent, "In A Mizz) is what I've come to expect will happen to any one of the songs written by Jack White for the White Stripes. In what feels like an affront to half of my existence (that rational, fact-obsessed robot), it's what I HOPE will happen, even if just once. Despite all best efforts, authorship will melt away, misattribution will overtake and long after our corporeal existence has atomized to dust, all that will be left is a couple of lines that transcend.

In life...the facts are there. The truth is attainable. It might be buried underneath eighty-some years of confusion and unintended obfuscation, but if you put in the work you can find it. There's a beauty to that. But there's hardly any romance there.

I don't know if the impetus for "I'm Finding It Harder To Be A Gentleman" is something real or an imagined figment. I hope Jack will take that one

---

9 Though the quote is from 2001, *Rolling Stone* did not print it until 2003. In this instance Jack refers to the song by the wrong title which only muddies the waters even further. "There's a song in the film, 'It Can't Be Love Because There Is No True Love' at a party they have in the Everglades. I was trying to play it on guitar and I went through the film and started writing down things that might rhyme and make sense together."—Jack White, *Rolling Stone*, April 1st, 2003

to the grave. But that girlfriend who I was hoping to impress with my door opening some twenty-two years ago? She's my wife now. These days I don't open her door nearly as much as I used to. But when I do, it easily makes her day.

Ben Blackwell
Official White Stripes archivist / historian / door-opener

STRANGE PILGRIM

by Caroline Randall Williams

I was late to the party.

The longer words are really breaking my back now—

In June of 2007 I was a walking, talking, Muddy Waters song—*nineteen years old, and got ways just like a baby child.* I was naive and lively and drunk on water bottle Jack Daniels after three days with a bunch of white kids in just about the dustiest field in Tennessee. I was at Bonnaroo, and ready to go home, but my friends *had* to see the White Stripes. So I stayed. I knew I was in for something, but I didn't know what. And I left that day still not knowing what, not knowing shit, really. Just like the girl in the song. I'd just buried my father the summer before, and I couldn't tell you where I was going, and there was nothing anyone could do to please me; I couldn't be satisfied. I was nineteen years old and I didn't know anything about the White Stripes.

But I do know now that I might not be here without them.

Finding it harder to be a gentleman—

Let me put it another way.

I think Jack White might have saved my life.

I discovered *Icky Thump* in 2012, when I was trying to leave a man. There'd been a lot of big emotions, a lot of psychological violence, a lot of physical chemistry and a lot of general chaos. He cooked beautifully. He had excellent taste in music. He was good at things bodies do together. He felt things intensely, and took too many pills. He was jealous all the time, and he kept a loaded gun under our bed.

I don't know how much of how long I stayed could be tied to which deadly sin—lust, gluttony, pride—or maybe it was all of all of them. Like I said, I don't know. I do know that I couldn't and wouldn't leave him without a reason, and that I couldn't, or wouldn't, find one. And I thought that was love.

Then the night before my twenty-fifth birthday, he raised a hand to me, and I screamed for help, and everything changed. I called the cops and I called my mama and I let my heart break every day for I don't know how long, thinking I'd turned my back on myself for letting it get like this. Thinking I'd turned my back on love for letting him go after all that.

And then someone—I don't remember who—played me "You Don't Know What Love Is, You Just Do As You're Told," and it gave me my life back.

It became an anthem. I had a respectable side. I didn't run and hide from anybody's pushing, or pulling, or pressure. That's how I missed the catastrophe for so long—I didn't just think I was strong, I knew it. Like the song says. I wasn't hopeless, or helpless. Like the song says. But that song, it knew something else, too. I love yous don't mean anything if you don't know how love works.

> *Till you realize you deserve better, I'm gonna lay right in to you.*

On repeat. The White Stripes a shield and a weapon for my sense of self somehow. You can't make this shit up. A Black girl from Tennessee listening to a man who took and kept his wife's last name to get her head straight in Mississippi. Goddamn.

It's wild and somehow fitting that a white boy from Detroit saved my life before I met him.

My mom was born in the Motor City. Her father had moved there as a boy, moved to escape white men and guns and danger in the deep south, and to find some joy, some real prosperity.

History is like a fussy old lady, the way she repeats herself sometimes.

> *Well, you're in your little room and you're working on something good*
> *But if it's really good, you're gonna need a bigger room*
> *And when you're in the bigger room, you might not know what to do*
> *You might have to think of how you got started sitting in your little room*

It's no secret that music can save your life. And that life saving that happened for me in Mississippi, it turned into a long love far beyond any one place or moment or personal chapter. I got this giant gift of a band and a body of work that, for all intents and purposes, had already happened. I found the White Stripes with their history already in place and waiting for me to come and see. Come and hear.

What I found was music that is fun and scary and dirty and weirdly sweet. The wishes in it pure and wistful and somehow existing fruitfully in the space between youthful angst and legitimate, justified, and justifiable rage. What an excellent, transcendent amalgam.

Whatever it is, they already said it.

> *Nothing could be better / Than hanging on the line / And waiting for an honest word forever—*

How else do I put this? How do I talk about the words on these pages without first starting a big picture conversation about what art is supposed to do? Like Jack, I am a poet who knows that sometimes you turn to other poets when you need the right words. So in a wild pivot, let me take you for a moment to Stalin's Russia, with a poet called Anna Akhmatova. In *Requiem*, her collection about the horrors of living through that time, she shares a memory, in lieu of a preface:

> During the terrifying years of the Yezhov repressions, I spent seventeen months in Leningrad prison lines. One time, someone thought they recognized me. Then a woman standing behind me, who of course had never heard my name, stirred from her own, though common to all of us, stupor and asked in my ear (there, all spoke in a whisper):
> —Could you describe this?
> And I said:
> —I can.
> Then, something akin to a smile slipped across what once had been her face.
>
> April 1, 1957, Leningrad

That moment has always sounded a lot to me like, *Can I get a witness?* The canonical question of the black church. The Blues Church. I mean the soul church. I mean the secularly sacred call of the Capital B, Capital C church of what's good, what delivers you TO heaven or what delivers you ON earth—*Can I get a witness*?

When you're an artist, the question shifts slightly. The question becomes, can I *be* a witness?

Can I tell it so that it rings right to the others who've lived it? Can I offer that precious relief that comes with feeling seen and not alone?

The act of witnessing is not just a respite. It's a balm against injustice. We make art to show we've lived, and how.

So yeah, I found the White Stripes about a decade late, while living in Mississippi, and they became an anchor, and a soundtrack—a train out of town.

During my first year of graduate school at the University in Oxford—I try never to call the school Ole Miss, that's a slave master's wife, not an alma mater, but I digress — I had the opportunity to go to Los Angeles for an event. I remember being in a car driving past film studios and saying to my mother, *This place reminds me in a way of Mississippi.* She looked at me with incredulity, a kind of real wonder. And I clarified. *In LA, it feels like anything is possible. Like, if you dream it, you could bring it to life, on screen. There's a magic in that.* In *Mississippi, it feels like anything could happen. Life or death or a ghost or a gift or a wild animal or some crisis wind or some miracle could be around any corner. Every second of every day is like that—and there's even more magic in it.*

Mississippi filled me with wonder because it's the best and worst of this country, all the time, and there's no way to hide from either side of it. The terrible systemic inequities, the ridiculous weather, the living things that will consume the house from under you, the relative lawlessness that means any backroad is a chaos highway for good or ill.

You need the right music to survive a thing like that. You need the right art to survive a thing like that. I love lists. I love putting things on repeat. White Stripes. Witnessing. Transcendence.

You fell down of course, and then you got up of course, and started over—

By the end of my time in Mississippi, I could barely listen to music anymore. I had to blast television at all hours of the day and night to cope with the deep-south sensory overload, to counter it somehow. Netflix recommended this then-obscure show, *Peaky Blinders*. Finally, I was an early adopter. At the party before anyone knew there was one. I watched season one over and over and over again. And slowly, after the smoke and the guns and the war stories and the booze and the sex got quiet in my head from the repetition, the show's soundtrack hit me, and I finally registered that familiar heartbeat; the White Stripes *all through* that show, the backbone of my favorite scenes, again giving my respite, my sense of self and safety, a sound with some good grit, with some *thump* in it.

Let's have a ball, girl, and take our sweet little time about it—

Now, years later, reading the lyrics, black on the white pages, is a different thing altogether. The tension that aches you and strains you when the drums tell your heart how to pulse the blood different and the guitar tells your mind how to race and the tight wail of Jack's voice sets your teeth on some cathartic edge, well, obviously, all of that falls away. And what you're left with is the bones, the proof of life artifacts that have become their own precious, separate thing. Pilgrims go to the relics to touch some certain, earthly piece of what they believe has delivered them, or will deliver them, from the troubles of this world. That's what this book is—these pages a pilgrimage. Come touch the bones of a thing that gives you life.

II

THE LYRICS

The White Stripes

1. JIMMY THE EXPLODER 27

2. STOP BREAKING DOWN (written by Robert Johnson)

3. THE BIG THREE KILLED MY BABY 29

4. SUZY LEE 31

5. SUGAR NEVER TASTED SO GOOD 33

6. WASTING MY TIME 35

7. CANNON 37

8. ASTRO 39

9. BROKEN BRICKS (lyrics by Stephen Gillis) 43

10. WHEN I HEAR MY NAME 45

11. DO 47

12. SCREWDRIVER 49

13. ONE MORE CUP OF COFFEE (written by Bob Dylan)

14. LITTLE PEOPLE 51

15. SLICKER DRIPS 53

16. ST. JAMES INFIRMARY BLUES (Traditional)

17. I FOUGHT PIRANHAS 55

JIMMY THE EXPLODER

Now, Jimmy
Well, do you want an explosion now?
Yeah, Jimmy
Do you want to explode now?
Yeah, monkey
Are you seeing red now?
Yeah, monkey
Jumping on the bed now

Green apples
On the tree and growing now
Green apples
Are gonna be exploding now
Yeah, monkey
Are you seeing red now?
Yeah, monkey
Jumping on the bed now

THE BIG THREE KILLED MY BABY

The Big Three killed my baby
No money in my hand again
The Big Three killed my baby
Nobody's coming home again

Their ideas make me want to spit
A hundred dollars goes down the pit
Thirty-thousand wheels are rolling
And my stick shift hands are swollen
Everything involved is shady
The Big Three killed my baby
The Big Three killed my baby
No money in my hand again
The Big Three killed my baby
Nobody's coming home again

Why don't you take the day off and try to repair?
A billion others don't seem to care
Better ideas are stuck in the mud
The motor's running on Tucker's blood
Don't let 'em tell you the future's electric
'Cause gasoline's not measured in metric
Thirty-thousand wheels are spinning
And oil company faces are grinning
Now my hands are turning red
And I found out my baby is dead
The Big Three killed my baby
No money in my hand again
The Big Three killed my baby
Nobody's coming home again

Well, I've said it now, nothing's changed
People are burning for pocket change
And creative minds are lazy
And the Big Three killed my baby

And my baby's my common sense
So don't feed me planned obsolescence
Yeah, my baby's my common sense
So don't feed me planned obsolescence (yeah)
I'm about to have another blow-out
I'm about to have another blow-out

SUZY LEE

There's a story
I would like to tell
My problem is
It's one you know too well
It's one you know too well

Miss Suzy Lee
The one I'm speaking of
The question is
Is she the one I love?
Is she the one I love? (alright)

Is she the one I love?
Is she the one I love?

She sent me flowers
With her tears burned inside
And you know what I'd do
I would run and hide
I would run and hide

And the paper
On it was my name
With the question
Do you feel the same?
Do you feel the same? (alright)

To end this tale
The one I'm speaking of
I wish I had an answer but I just don't know
Is this really love?
Is this really love?

Is this really love?
Is this really love?

SUGAR NEVER TASTED SO GOOD

Sugar never tasted so good
Sugar never tasted so good
Sugar never tasted good to me
Until her eyes crossed over
Until her mind crossed over
Until her soul fell next to me

Now
If the wrinkle that is in your brain
Has given you quite a sting
Your fingers have become a crane
Pulling on these puppet strings
What a feeling that's begun
What a feeling that's begun
What a feeling that's begun
What a feeling that's begun

Alright
I felt just like a baby
Until I held a baby
What a fool this boy can be
And her thoughts like a daisy's
How my mind gets lazy
I must have been crazy not to see
If the wrinkle that is in your brain
Has given you quite a sting
Your fingers have become a crane
Your fingers have become a crane
Your fingers have become a crane
Pulling on these puppet strings

Water never tasted so good
Water never tasted so good
Water never tasted good to me

WASTING MY TIME

And if I'm wasting my time
Then nothing could be better
Than hanging on the line
And waiting for an honest word forever

And if you're saying goodbye
Please don't you think me bitter
For recalling every rhyme
From the book, the page, the line, the word, the letter

Well, the window's turning blue
And the waters ever flowing
And I hope I'm not a fool
For laughing at myself as you were going

CANNON

Outside
My door
Unlocked
I'm lookin'
At this sound
That chime out of nowhere
Yeah, nowhere

Wheels turnin'
Scratching
And burnin'
I saw guns
Tanks
Cannon
Cannon

Tell me who's that writin'
John the Revelator
Tell me who's that writin'
John the Revelator
Who's that writin'

John the Revelator wrote the book of the Seven Seals

Christ went down on Easter mornin'
Mary n' Martha went down to see
"Go tell my disciples, to meet me in Galilee"

Who's the writer?
John the Revelator
Tell me who's that writin'
John the Revelator
Tell me who's that writer
John the Revelator wrote the book of the Seven Seals
Yeah

Lord above
How can man
Be evil?
Evil
Evil

ASTRO

Maybe Jasper does the astro
Maybe Jasper does the astro
Maybe Jasper does the astro, astro
Maybe Lily does the astro
Maybe Lily does the astro
Maybe Lily does the astro, astro
Maybe Jackson does the astro
Maybe Jackson does the astro
Maybe Jackson does the astro, astro
Maybe mama does the astro
Maybe mama does the astro
Maybe mama does the astro, astro
Well, maybe Tesla does the astro
Maybe Tesla does the astro
Maybe Edison is AC/DC

BROKEN BRICKS (lyrics by Stephen Gillis)

Well, have you been to the broken bricks, girl
Snuck down through the cyclone fence
Past the caution tape and the security gate
Backwards to the breakroom bench
Well, there's a little corner where you first got kissed
And felt her boyfriend's fist and made the company list
And there's a little spot where your dad ate lunch
And your brother landed his first punch

Well have you been to the broken bricks, girl
Seen the barrels that they left behind?
Seen the machine that cut aluminium clean
Duct tape on the caution sign
Broken tooth window panes
Drip a rusty-colored rain that drives a man insane
You try to jump over water but you land in oil
Climb the metal of a broken crane

Don't go to the broken bricks, girl
It's not the place that you want to be
Think about the spot your father spent his life
Demolition calls it building "C"
Demolition calls it building "C," now
Demolition calls it building "C," now

WHEN I HEAR MY NAME

When I hear my name I want to disappear
When I see my face I want to disappear
When I see my face I want to disappear
When I hear my name I want to disappear

DO

Well, somebody walked up to me
But I didn't know what to do
And then somebody said hello to me
But I didn't know what to do
Because I think that my words could get
Twisted so I bend my back over take a
Gulp be funny cause I know there's nothing I can do

Then my mother tried to pick me up
'Cause I was sitting down on the ground
Something forced my little eyes come open
But I couldn't make out the sound
It doesn't matter cause my eyes are lying
And they don't have emotion
Don't wanna be social
Can't take it when they hate me
But I know there's nothing I can do

When my thoughts start to feel like mine
They're taken from me, it seems to happen every time
And the feelings that are fine for you
There's somebody there
Who doesn't think they are true
So think of something new
There's nothing left to do

And then my idols walk next to me
I look up at them they fade away
It's a destruction of a mystery
The more I listen to what they say
So does that mean that there's no more doing
And there's no more thinking
And there's no more feeling
Cause there's no right opinion
Can you tell me what I'm supposed to do

SCREWDRIVER

Tuesday morning now
I gotta have somewhere to go
I call up Tommy now
I call him on the telephone
Won't you wake up and come with me now
I'm going to the pawn and loan
Walking down thirty three
Walking down thirty oh

Well, what am I supposed to think
I drop a nickel in the sink
I love people like a brother now
But I'm not gonna be their mother now
What if someone walked up to me
And like an apple cut right through me
I'm not just gonna stand there grinning
Cuz I'm not the one who's sinnin'
Screwdriver

Now that you have heard my story now
I've got a little ending to it now
Whenever you go out alone
Take a little dog a bone
Think about your little sister
Then you got to drive it home
Screwdriver

I got a little feeling goin' now
Now Now Now

LITTLE PEOPLE

There's a little girl who says bing bing bop
There's a little girl who says bing bing bop, hello
There's a little boy with a spider in his hand
There's a little boy with a spider in his hand, hello

There's a little girl with the red shoes on
There's a little girl with the red shoes on, hello
There's a little boy with twenty five cents
There's a little boy with twenty five cents, hello

And there's a little girl with a tiger on her bed
There's a little girl with a tiger on her bed, hello
There's a little boy with nothin' on his mind
There's a little boy with nothin' on his mind, hello

SLICKER DRIPS

They're lookin' at me
No where to go
And what they're sayin'
Just don't know
A floor below me
A ceiling above
And I'm in the middle
With nobody to love
Nobody to love
Nobody to love
Nobody to love

They're lookin' at me
Nowhere to go
I hear what they're sayin'
I just don't know
With a floor below you now
A ceiling above
You're in the middle
With nobody to love
Nobody to love

I FOUGHT PIRANHAS

Well, I hold the rope
And I hold the sail
And I kept my papers
To keep from land in jail
And I fought piranhas
And I fought the cold
There was no one with me
I was all alone

Well, it's Easter morning now
And there's no one around
So I unroll the cement
And walk into the town
There was no one with me
I was all alone
And I fought piranhas
And I fought the cold

Well, you know what it's like
I don't got to tell you
Who puts up a fight
Walking out of hell now
When you fought piranhas
And you fought the cold
There's nobody with you
Yes, you're all alone

De Stijl

1. YOU'RE PRETTY GOOD LOOKING (FOR A GIRL) 59
2. HELLO OPERATOR 61
3. LITTLE BIRD 63
4. APPLE BLOSSOM 65
5. I'M BOUND TO PACK IT UP 67
6. DEATH LETTER (written by Son House)
7. SISTER, DO YOU KNOW MY NAME? 69
8. TRUTH DOESN'T MAKE A NOISE 73
9. A BOY'S BEST FRIEND 75
10. LET'S BUILD A HOME 77
11. JUMBLE, JUMBLE 79
12. WHY CAN'T YOU BE NICER TO ME? 81
13. YOUR SOUTHERN CAN IS MINE (written by Blind Willie McTell)

YOU'RE PRETTY GOOD LOOKING (FOR A GIRL)

Oh yeah, you're pretty good looking... for a girl
But your back is so broken
And this feeling's still gonna linger on
Until the year 2525 now

Yeah, you're pretty good looking... for a girl
Your eyes are wide open
And your thoughts have been stolen by the boys
Who took you out and bought you everything you own now

Yeah, you're pretty good looking
You're pretty good looking
Yes, you're pretty good looking
For a girl

Lots of people in this world
But I wanna be your boy
To me, that thought is sounding so absurd
And I don't wanna be your toy

'Cause you're pretty good looking... for a girl
My future's wide open
But this feeling's still gonna linger on
Until I know everything I need to know now

Yeah, you're pretty good looking
You're pretty good looking
Yes, you're pretty good looking
For a girl

HELLO OPERATOR

Hello, operator
Can you give me number nine?
Can I see you later?
Will you give me back my dime?
Turn the oscillator
Twist it with a dollar bill
Mailman, bring the paper
Leave it on my window sill

Find a canary
A bird to bring my message home
Carry my obituary
My coffin doesn't have a phone
How you gonna get the money?
Send papers to an empty home?
How you gonna get the money?
Nobody to answer the phone

LITTLE BIRD

I got a little bird
I'm gonna take her home
Put her in a cage
And disconnect the phone

If you give me a look
I'm gonna get the book
I'm gonna preach the word
I wanna preach to birds
As I walk the floor
Yeah, this I know

When I get you home
This is how it goes
I got nothing to lose
I'll never let you go

APPLE BLOSSOM

Hey, little apple blossom
What seems to be the problem?
All the ones you tell your troubles to
They don't really care for you
Come and tell me what you're thinking
'Cause just when the boat is sinking
A little light is blinking
And I will come and rescue you

Lots of girls walk around in tears
But that's not for you
You've been looking all around for years
For someone to tell your troubles to

Come and sit with me and talk awhile
Let me see your pretty little smile
Put your troubles in a little pile
And I will sort 'em out for you

Lots of girls walk around in tears
But that's not for you
You've been looking all around for years
For someone to tell your troubles to

Come and sit with me and talk awhile
Let me see your pretty little smile
Put your troubles in a little pile
And I will sort them out for you

I'll fall in love with you
I think I'll marry you

I'M BOUND TO PACK IT UP

I've thought about it for awhile
And I've thought about the many miles
But I think it's time that I've gone away
The feelings that you have for me
Have gone away it's plain to see
And it looks to me that you're pulling away

I'm gonna pick it up
I'm gonna pick it up today
I'm bound to pack it up
I'm bound to pack it up and go away

I find it hard to say to you
That this is what I have to do
But there is no way that I'm gonna stay
There are so many things you need to know
And I wanna tell you before I go
But it's hard to think of just what to say

I'm gonna pick it up
I'm gonna pick it up today
I'm bound to pack it up
I'm bound to pack it up and go away

I'm sorry to leave you all alone
You're sitting silent by the phone
But we'd always known there would come a day
The bus is warm and softly lit
And a hundred people ride in it
I guess I'm just another running away

I'm gonna pick it up
I'm gonna pick it up today
I'm bound to pack it up
I'm bound to pack it up and go away

SISTER, DO YOU KNOW MY NAME?

Well, we're back in school again
And I don't really know anyone
I really wanna be your friend
'Cause I don't really know anyone
And the bus is pulling up to your house
I wish you could be sitting here next to me

I didn't see you at summer school
But I saw you at the corner store
And I don't want to break the rules
'Cause I've broken them all before
But every time I see you, I wonder why
I don't break a couple rules so that you'll notice me

Sister, do you know my name?
I've heard it before but I wanna know
I got a funny feeling that it's gonna work out
'Cause now I see you sitting here next to me

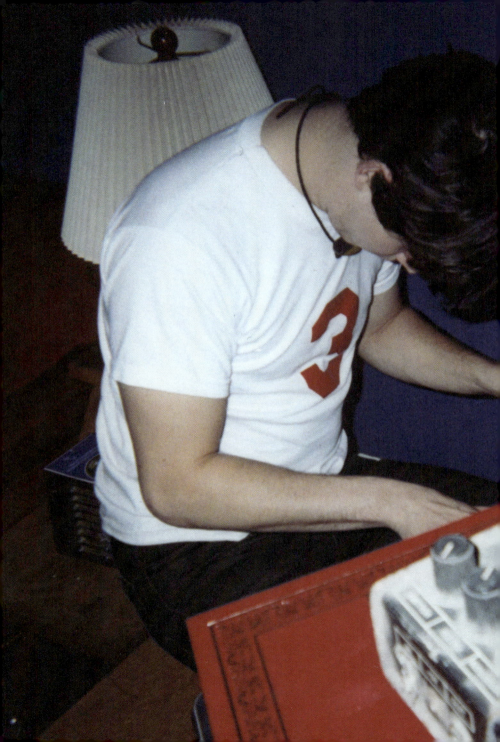

TRUTH DOESN'T MAKE A NOISE

My baby's got a heart of stone
Can't you people just leave her alone?
She never did nothin' to hurt you
So just leave her alone
The motion of her tiny hands
And the quiver of her bones below
Are the signs of a girl alone
And tell you everything you need to know

I can't explain it
I feel it often
Every time I see her face
But the way you treat her
Fills me with rage and I wanna tear apart the place

You try to tell her what to do
And all she does is stare at you
Her stare is louder than your voice
Because truth doesn't make a noise
No—truth doesn't make a noise
Truth doesn't make a noise

I can't explain it
I feel it often
Every time I see her face
But the way you treat her, it fills me with rage and I want to tear apart
the place

You're Pretty Good Looking
When I Hear My Name
Truth Doesn't Make A Noise
Wasting My Time
Astro
Little Bird
Stop Breaking → Down
Lafayette Blues
CANNON
ONE MORE CUP OF COFFEE
Jimmy The Exploder
Southern Can
Apple Blossom
Lets Shake Hands

A BOY'S BEST FRIEND

I just don't fit in this place
Their thoughts cast me out of here
Their home has run out of space
My mind's already out of here

Won't you come along, dear?
Won't you come along?

Words that are spoke alone
Phrases you will never hear
Empty rooms and a telephone
That I will never use, never fear

I am all alone, dear
I am all alone

My dogs come sit next to me
A pack of dogs and cigarettes
My only friends speak no words to me
But they look at me and they don't forget
That a boy's best friend is his mother or whatever has become his pet

LET'S BUILD A HOME

Some bricks now, baby
Say, let's build a home
Some bricks now, baby
Say, let's build a home

I'm getting lazy
Won't you throw me a bone?
I'm getting lazy
Won't you throw me a bone?

Some bricks now, baby
Say, let's build a home
Some bricks now, baby
Say, let's build a home

JUMBLE, JUMBLE

Jumble, jumble
All at my house
Come on over
Sleep on the couch
Can't even see ya
Look like a mouse

Crumble, crumble
That bag is brown
Rip up the paper
To hear a sound
Pick the pieces
Up off the ground

Tumble, tumble
Onto the floor
Roll over
Until you're poor
Wave to me
I'm at the door

WHY CAN'T YOU BE NICER TO ME?

Somebody's screaming
Looking at the ceiling
Everything's so funny
I don't have any money
People don't even know me
But they know how to show me

Why can't you be nicer to me?

My pride is dying
I think I'm all done lying
Nobody's sharing
So I stopped caring
All alone and walking
Nobody's talking

Why can't you be nicer to me?

Well, the wind is blowing
Where am I going?
Off a bridge and falling
Nobody's calling
On the ground and laying
Nobody's praying

Why can't you be nicer to me?

White Blood Cells

1. DEAD LEAVES AND THE DIRTY GROUND 85

2. HOTEL YORBA 87

3. I'M FINDING IT HARDER TO BE A GENTLEMAN 89

4. FELL IN LOVE WITH A GIRL 91

5. EXPECTING 93

6. LITTLE ROOM 95

7. THE UNION FOREVER 97

8. THE SAME BOY YOU'VE ALWAYS KNOWN 99

9. WE'RE GOING TO BE FRIENDS 101

10. OFFEND IN EVERY WAY 103

11. I THINK I SMELL A RAT 105

12. ALUMINUM

13. I CAN'T WAIT 107

14. NOW MARY 109

15. I CAN LEARN 111

16. THIS PROTECTOR 113

DEAD LEAVES AND THE DIRTY GROUND

Dead leaves and the dirty ground
When I know you're not around
Shiny tops and soda pops
When I hear your lips make a sound
When I hear your lips make a sound
Thirty notes in the mailbox
Will tell you that I'm coming home
And I think I'm gonna stick around
For a while so you're not alone
For a while so you're not alone

If you can hear a piano fall
You can hear me coming down the hall
If I could just hear your pretty voice
I don't think I'd need to see at all
Don't think I'd need to see at all
Soft hair and a velvet tongue
I want to give you what you give to me
And every breath that is in your lungs
Is a tiny little gift to me
Is a tiny little gift to me

I didn't feel so bad 'til the sun went down
Then I come home
No one to wrap my arms around
Wrap my arms around

Well, any man with a microphone
Can tell you what he loves the most
And you know why you love at all
If you're thinking of the holy ghost
If you're thinking of the holy ghost

HOTEL YORBA

I was watching
With one eye on the other side
I had fifteen people telling me to move
I got moving on my mind
I found shelter
In some thoughts turning wheels around
I said 39 times that I love you
To the beauty I had found

Well, it's 1, 2, 3, 4
Take the elevator
At the Hotel Yorba
I'll be glad to see you later
All they got inside is vacancy

I been thinking
Of a little place down by the lake
They got a dirty old road leading up to the house
I wonder how long it will take 'til we're alone
Sitting on the front porch of that home
Stomping our feet on the wooden boards
Never gotta worry about locking the door

Well, it's 1, 2, 3, 4
Take the elevator
At the Hotel Yorba
I'll be glad to see you later
All they got inside is vacancy

It might sound silly
For me to think childish thoughts like these
But I'm so tired of acting tough
And I'm gonna do what I please
Let's get married
In a big cathedral by a priest

'Cause if I'm the man that you love the most
You could say 'I do' at least

Well, it's 1, 2, 3, 4
Take the elevator
At the Hotel Yorba
I'll be glad to see you later
All they got inside is vacancy

And it's 4, 5, 6, 7
Grab your umbrella
Grab hold of me
'Cause I'm your favorite fella
All they got inside is vacancy

I'M FINDING IT HARDER TO BE A GENTLEMAN

Well I'm finding it harder
To be a gentleman every day
All the manners that I've been taught
Have slowly died away
But if I held the door open for you
It would make your day

You think that I care
About me and only me
When every single girl needs help
Climbing up a tree
Well, I know it don't take much
To satisfy me

Maybe it's whatever is in my hand
That's distracting me
But if I could find emotion
To stimulate devotion
Well, then you'd see

Well, I'm finding it hard to say
That I need you twenty times a day
I feel comfortable so baby why
Don't you feel the same?
Have a doctor come and visit us
And tell us which one is sane

I'd never said I wouldn't
Throw my jacket in the mud for you
But my father gave it to me so
Maybe I should carry you
Then you said, "You almost dropped me"
So then I did
And I got mud on my shoes

FELL IN LOVE WITH A GIRL

Fell in love with a girl
I fell in love once and almost completely
She's in love with the world
But sometimes, these feelings can be so misleading
She turns and says, "Are you alright?"
I said, "I must be fine 'cause my heart's still beating."
"Come and kiss me by the riverside, yeah
Bobby says it's fine, he don't consider it cheating, now."

Red hair with a curl
Mello-Roll for the flavor, and the eyes were peeping
Can't keep away from the girl
These two sides of my brain need to have a meeting
Can't think of anything to do, yeah
My left brain knows that all love is fleeting
She's just looking for something new, yeah
I said it once before, but it bears repeating now

Can't think of anything to do, yeah
My left brain knows that all love is fleeting
She's just looking for something new
Well, I said it once before, but it bears repeating now

Fell in love with a girl
I fell in love once and almost completely
She's in love with the world
But sometimes, these feelings can be so misleading
She turns and says, "Are you alright?"
I said, "I must be fine because my heart's still beating."
"Come and kiss me by the riverside, yeah
Bobby says it's fine he don't consider it cheating, now."

Can't think of anything to do, yeah
My left brain knows that all love is fleeting
She's just looking for something new
Well, I said it once before, but it bears repeating now

EXPECTING

Your mouth said this never
But your fingers have shown me
Your head is so clever
You claim that you own me
Forever
Forever
Forever
Forever

You have the right to conduct me
In whatever fashion
Your attempt to construct me
In the interest of passion
You sent me
To Toledo
Toledo
Toledo

I came back with handfuls
I did what you asked me
But after the thank yous
That you quickly got past me
I'm expected
You're expecting
I'm expected
Expected

Can you go get me the…

LITTLE ROOM

Well, you're in your little room and you're working on something good
But if it's really good, you're gonna need a bigger room
And when you're in the bigger room, you might not know what to do
You might have to think of how you got started sitting in your little room

THE UNION FOREVER

It can't be love
For there is no true love
It can't be love
For there is no true love

Sure I'm C.F.K
But you gotta love me
The cost no man can say
But you gotta love me

Well, I'm sorry but I'm not
Interested in gold mines
Oil wells, shipping or real estate
What would I liked to have been?
Everything you hate

Cause it can't be love
For there is no true love
It can't be love
For there is no true love

There is a man
A certain man
And for the poor you may be sure
That he'll do all he can
Who is this one?
Whose favorite son?
Just by his action has the traction
Magnates on the run
Who likes to smoke?
Enjoys a joke?
And wouldn't get a bit
Upset if he were really broke?
With wealth and fame

He's still the same
I'll bet you five you're not alive
If you don't know his name

You said, the union forever
You said, the union forever
You cried, the union forever
But that was untrue, girl

'Cause it can't be love
For there is no true love
It can't be love
For there is no true love

THE SAME BOY YOU'VE ALWAYS KNOWN

You fell down of course
And then you got up of course
And started over
Forgot my name of course
Then you started to remember
Pretty tough to think about
The beginning of December

Pretty tough to think about
Pretty tough to think about
Pretty tough to think about

You're looking down again
And then you look me over
We're laying down again
On a blanket in the clover
The same boy you've always known
Well, I guess I haven't grown
The same boy you've always known
Same boy you've always known

Think of what the past did
It could've lasted
So put it in your basket
I hope you know a strong man
Who can lend you a hand
Lowering my casket

I thought this is just today
And soon you'd been returning
The coldest blue ocean water
Cannot stop my heart and mind
From burning
Everyone who's in the know says
That's exactly how it goes
And if there's anything good about me
I'm the only one who knows

WE'RE GOING TO BE FRIENDS

Fall is here, hear the yell
Back to school, ring the bell
Brand new shoes, walking blues
Climb the fence, books and pens
I can tell that we are going to be friends
I can tell that we are going to be friends

Walk with me, Suzy Lee
Through the park and by the tree
We will rest upon the ground
And look at all the bugs we found
Safely walk to school without a sound
Safely walk to school without a sound

Here we are, no one else
We walk to school all by ourselves
There's dirt on our uniforms
From chasing all the ants and worms
We clean up and now it's time to learn
We clean up and now it's time to learn

Numbers, letters, learn to spell
Nouns, and books, and show and tell
Playtime, we will throw the ball
Back to class, through the hall
Teacher marks our height against the wall
Teacher marks our height against the wall

And we don't notice any time pass
We don't notice anything
We sit side by side in every class
Teacher thinks that I sound funny
But she likes the way you sing
Tonight I'll dream, while I'm in bed
When silly thoughts go through my head

About the bugs and alphabet
And when I wake tomorrow, I'll bet
That you and I will walk together again

I can tell that we are going to be friends
Yes, I can tell that we are going to be friends

OFFEND IN EVERY WAY

I'm patient of this plan
As humble as I can
I'll wait another day
Before I turn away
But know this much is true
No matter what I do
Offend in every way
I don't know what to say

I'm coming through the door
But they're expecting more
Of an interesting man
Sometimes I think I can
But how much can I fake
I'll speak until I break
With every word I say
Offend in every way

You tell me to relax
And listen to these facts
That everyone's my friend
And will be till the end
But know this much is true
No matter what I do
No matter what I say
Offend in every way

I THINK I SMELL A RAT

I think I smell a rat
I think I smell a rat
All you little kids seem to think you know just where it's at
I think I smell a rat
Walking down the street carrying a baseball bat
I think I smell a rat

I think I smell a rat
I think I smell a rat
All you little kids seem to think you know just where it's at
I think I smell a rat
Using your mother and father for a welcome mat
I think I smell a rat

I CAN'T WAIT

I can't wait till you try to come back girl
When things they don't work out for you
Who do you think you're messing with girl
What do you think you're trying to do?

Who do you think you're messing with girl
What do you think you're trying to do?
Do you really think I want be left out girl
Who do you think you're trying to fool

First you said I was blind
And it's gonna be different this time
I thought you made up your mind
I thought you made up your mind
I thought you made up
I thought you made up
I thought you made up your mind

So many times I've gotten used to this
This old idea of being all alone
Tell me how I'm supposed to get through with this?
I wish this house felt like a home

Who do you think you're messing with girl
What do you think you're trying to do?
Do you really think I want be left out girl
Who do you think you're trying to fool

First you said I was blind
You certainly took your time
I thought you made up your mind
I thought you made up your mind
I thought you made up
I thought you made up
I thought you made up your mind

NOW MARY

Now, Mary
Can't you find a way
To bring me down?
I'm so sorry
That I had to go
And let you down

Knowing you I'll think things are gonna be fine
But then again you'll probably change your mind

I'm sorry, Mary, but being your mate
Means trying to find something that you aren't going to hate
What a season
To be beautiful
Without a reason

Knowing you I'll think things are gonna be fine
But then again you'll probably change your mind

Mary,
Can't you find a way to bring me down?

I CAN LEARN

I wish we were stuck up a tree
Then we'd know it's nicer below
I don't know any lullabies
I don't know how to make you mine
But I can learn
In lonely days long ago
I saw lovers put on a show
Well, now it's my turn

Drive you home then wait by the phone
For that call, for a walk in the fall
No harm will come of this
One little midnight kiss
It will not burn
So many lonely days
I feel like a throw-away
Well, now it's my turn

Falling down is no longer around
Feeling sun, I'm no longer one
Well, isn't this fun?

THIS PROTECTOR

I never thought that I had to be this protector
So many thoughts inside my head a strange collector

But now
But now
But now
Now, now, now, now, now

You thought you heard a sound
There's no one else around
Looking at the door
It's coming through the floor

300 people living out in West Virginia
Have no idea of all these thoughts that lie within ya

But now
But now
But now
Now, now, now, now, now

You thought you heard a sound
There's no one else around
Looking at the door
It's coming through the floor

Elephant

1. SEVEN NATION ARMY 117

2. BLACK MATH 119

3. THERE'S NO HOME FOR YOU HERE 121

4. I JUST DON'T KNOW WHAT TO DO WITH MYSELF (written by Burt Bacharach & Hal David)

5. IN THE COLD, COLD NIGHT 123

6. I WANT TO BE THE BOY TO WARM YOUR MOTHER'S HEART 125

7. YOU'VE GOT HER IN YOUR POCKET 127

8. BALL AND BISCUIT 129

9. THE HARDEST BUTTON TO BUTTON 131

10. LITTLE ACORNS 133

11. HYPNOTIZE 135

12. THE AIR NEAR MY FINGERS 137

13. GIRL, YOU HAVE NO FAITH IN MEDICINE 139

14. IT'S TRUE THAT WE LOVE ONE ANOTHER 14

SEVEN NATION ARMY

I'm gonna fight 'em off
A seven nation army couldn't hold me back
They're gonna rip it off
Taking their time right behind my back
And I'm talking to myself at night
Because I can't forget
Back and forth through my mind
Behind a cigarette

And the message coming from my eyes
Says, "Leave it alone"

Don't want to hear about it
Every single one's got a story to tell
Everyone knows about it
From the Queen of England to the hounds of hell
And if I catch it coming back my way
I'm gonna serve it to you
And that ain't what you want to hear
But that's what I'll do

And the feeling coming from my bones
Says, "Find a home"

I'm going to Wichita
Far from this opera for evermore
I'm gonna work the straw
Make the sweat drip out of every pore
And I'm bleeding, and I'm bleeding, and I'm bleeding
Right before the Lord
All the words are gonna bleed from me
And I will think no more

And the stains coming from my blood
Tell me, "Go back home"

BLACK MATH

Don't you think that I'm bound to react now?
Well, my fingers definitely turning to black now
Yeah, well, maybe I'll put my love on ice
Teach myself, maybe that'll be nice

My books are sitting at the top of the stack now
The longer words are really breaking my back now
Maybe I'll learn to understand
Drawing a square with a pencil in hand

Mathematically turning the page
Unequivocally showing my age
I'm practically center stage
Undeniably earning your wage
Well, maybe I'll put my love on ice
And teach myself, maybe that'll be nice

Listen master, can you answer a question?
Is it the fingers, or the brain
That you're teaching a lesson?
I can't tell you how proud I am
I'm writing down things that I don't understand

Well, maybe I'll put my love on ice
And teach myself, maybe that'll be nice

THERE'S NO HOME FOR YOU HERE

There's no home for you here, girl, go away
There's no home for you here
There's no home for you here, girl, go away
There's no home for you here

I'd like to think that all of this constant interaction
Is just the kind to make you drive yourself away
Each simple gesture done by me is counteracted
And leaves me standing here with nothing else to say
Completely baffled by a backward indication
That an inspired word will come across your tongue
Hands moving upward to propel the situation
Have simply halted
Now the conversation's done

There's no home for you here, girl, go away
There's no home for you here
There's no home for you here, girl, go away
There's no home for you here

I'm only waiting for the proper time to tell you
That it's impossible to get along with you
It's hard to look you in the face when we are talking
So it helps to have a mirror in the room
I've not been really looking forward to the performance
But there's my cue and there's a question on your face
Fortunately I have come across an answer
Which is go away
And do not leave a trace

There's no home for you here, girl, go away
There's no home for you here
There's no home for you here, girl, go away
There's no home for you here

Waking up for breakfast
Burning matches
Talking quickly
Breaking baubles
Throwing garbage
Drinking soda
Looking happy
Taking pictures
So completely stupid
Just go away

There's no home for you here, girl, go away
There's no home for you here
There's no home for you here, girl, go away
No home here

There's no home for you here, girl, go away
There's no home for you here
There's no home for you here, girl, go away
There's no home for you here

IN THE COLD, COLD NIGHT

I saw you standing in the corner
On the edge of a burning light
I saw you standing in the corner

Come to me again in the cold, cold night

You make me feel a little older
Like a full grown woman might
But when you're gone I grow colder

Come to me again in the cold, cold night

I hear you walking by my front door
I hear the creaking of the kitchen floor
I don't care what other people say
I'm going to love you, anyway

Come to me again in the cold, cold night

I can't stand it any longer
I need the fuel to make my fire bright
So don't fight it any longer

Come to me again in the cold, cold night

And I know that you feel it too
When my skin turns into glue
You will know that it's warm inside
And you'll come run to me
In the cold, cold night

I WANT TO BE THE BOY TO WARM YOUR MOTHER'S HEART

I want to be the boy to warm your mother's heart
I'm so scared to take you away
I tried to win her over right from the start
But something always got in the way
We've been sitting in your backyard for hours
But she won't even come out and say hi
While my mother baked a little cake for you
And even dreaded when you said goodbye

What kind of cartwheels do I have to pull?
What kind of joke should I lay on her now?
I'm inclined to go finish high school
Just to make her notice that I'm around

Well, nothing I come up with seems to work
It feels like everything I say is a lie
And never have I felt like such a jerk
I'm afraid to even open my eyes
Because I really don't want her to judge me
I want her to really know who I am
And then and only then, will she love me
Well, at least that was the plan
If ever a boy needed a holiday
If ever a girl needed someone to hold
I just hope I don't act the same way
By the time that I get that old

What kind of cartwheels do I have to pull?
What kind of joke should I lay on her now?
I'm inclined to go finish high school
Just to make her notice that I'm around

I never said I was an heir to a fortune
I never claimed to have any looks
But these kind of things must be important
'Cause somebody ripped out my page in your telephone book
I want to warm her heart

YOU'VE GOT HER IN YOUR POCKET

You've got her in your pocket
And there's no way out now
Put it in the safe and lock it
'Cause it's home sweet home

Nobody ever told you that it was the wrong way
To trick a woman, make her feel she did it her way
And you'll be there if she ever feels blue
And you'll be there when she finds someone new
What to do?
Well, you know

You keep her in your pocket
Where there's no way out now
Put it in the safe and lock it
'Cause it's home sweet home

The smile on your face made her think she had the right one
And she thought she was sure by the way you two could have fun
But now she might leave like she's threatened before
Grab hold of her fast before her feet leave the floor
And she's out the door
'Cause you want

To keep her in your pocket
Where there's no way out now
Put it in the safe and lock it
'Cause it's home sweet home

And in your own mind, you know you're lucky just to know her
And in the beginning all you wanted was to show her
But now you're scared, you think she's running away
You search in your hand for something clever to say;
"Don't go away"
'Cause I want

To keep you in my pocket
Where there's no way out now
Put it in the safe and lock it
'Cause it's home sweet home

Home sweet home

BALL AND BISCUIT

It's quite possible that I'm your third man, girl
But it's a fact that I'm the seventh son
It's quite possible that I'm your third man, girl
But it's a fact that I'm the seventh son
And right now, you could care less about me
But soon enough, you will care by the time I'm done

Let's have a ball and a biscuit, sugar
And take our sweet little time about it
Let's have a ball, girl
And take our sweet little time about it
Tell everybody in the place to just get out
We'll get clean together
And I'll find me a soapbox where I can shout it

Now read it in the newspaper
Ask your girlfriends and see if they know
Read it in the newspaper
Ask your girlfriends and see if they know
That my strength is ten fold, girl
I'll let you see it if you want to before you go

Let's have a ball and a biscuit, sugar
And take our sweet little time about it
Let's have a ball
And take our sweet little time about it
Tell everybody in the place to just get out
We'll get clean together
And I'll find me a soapbox where I can shout it
And I can think of one or two things to say about it
Alright, listen
Alright, you get the point now?

It's quite possible that I'm your third man
But it's a fact that I'm the seventh son

It was the other two which made me your third
But it's my mother who made me the seventh son
And right now, you could care less about me
But soon enough, you will care by the time I'm done

Yeah, you just wait
You stick around
You'll figure it out

THE HARDEST BUTTON TO BUTTON

We started living in an old house
My ma gave birth and we were checking it out
It was a baby boy, so we bought him a toy
It was a ray gun, and it was 1981

We named him 'Baby'
He had a toothache
He started crying, it sounded like an earthquake
It didn't last long, because I stopped it
I grabbed a rag doll and stuck some little pins in it

Now we're a family, and we're alright now
We got money, and a little place to fight now
We don't know you, and we don't owe you
But if you see us around, I got something else to show you

Now it's easy when you don't know better
You think it's sleazy? Then put it in a short letter
We keep warm, but there's just something wrong with you
Just feel that you're the hardest little button to button

I had opinions that didn't matter
I had a brain that felt like pancake batter
I got a backyard with nothing in it
Except a stick, a dog, and a box with something in it

The hardest button to button
The hardest button to button
The hardest button to button
The hardest button to button
Uh-oh

LITTLE ACORNS

(Spoken word by Mort Crim)
When problems overwhelm us and sadness smothers us, where do we find the will and the courage to continue? Well, the answer may come in the caring voice of a friend, a chance encounter with a book, or from a personal faith. For Janet, help came from her faith, but it also came from a squirrel. Shortly after her divorce, Janet lost her father then she lost her job, she had mounting money problems. But Janet not only survived, she worked her way out of despondency and now she says, life is good again. How could this happen? She told me that late one autumn day when she was at her lowest, she watched a squirrel storing up nuts for the winter, one at a time he would take them to the nest. And she thought, if that squirrel can take care of himself with a harsh winter coming on, so can I. Once I broke my problems into small pieces, I was able to carry them, just like those acorns, one at a time

Take all your problems and rip 'em apart
Carry them off in a shopping cart
Another thing you should've known from the start
The problems in hand are lighter than at heart

Be like the squirrel, girl, be like the squirrel
Give it a whirl, girl, be like the squirrel
And another thing you have to know in this world
Cut up your hair, straighten your curls
Well, your problems hide in your curls

HYPNOTIZE

I want to hypnotize you, baby, on the telephone
So many times I called your house just to hear the tone
And though I knew that you weren't home
I didn't mind so much cause I'm so alone
I want to hypnotize you, baby, on the telephone

I want to spin my little watch right before your eyes
You're the kind of girl a guy like me could hypnotize
And if this comes as a surprise
Just think of all those guys that would tell you lies
I want to spin my little watch right before your eyes

I want to hold your little hand if I can be so bold
And be your right hand man 'til your hands get old
Then when all the feeling's gone
Just decide if you want to keep holding on
I want to hold your little hand if I can be so bold

If I can be so bold
If I can be so bold

THE AIR NEAR MY FINGERS

Life is so boring
It's really got me snoring
I'm wearing out the flooring in a cheap motel
But I don't have to work and
I might be sinning
But I'm never gonna have to hear the rings of school bells

Don't you remember?
You told me in December
That a boy is not a man until he makes a stand
Well, I'm not a genius
But maybe you'll remember this
I never said I ever wanted to be a man

I get nervous when she comes around
When she comes around, when she comes around
I get nervous when she comes around
When she comes around, when she comes around
I get nervous when she comes around
When she comes around, when she comes around
I get nervous when she comes around
When she comes around, when she comes around

My mom is so caring
She's really got me staring
At all the crazy little things she does for sure
And I can't seem to think of
Another kind of love
That a boy could ever get from anyone but her

I get nervous when she comes around
When she comes around, when she comes around
I get nervous when she comes around
When she comes around, when she comes around
I get nervous when she comes around

When she comes around, when she comes around
I get nervous when she comes around
When she comes around, when she comes around

GIRL, YOU HAVE NO FAITH IN MEDICINE

Girl, you have no faith in medicine
Oh girl, you have no faith in medicine
Acetaminophen, you see the medicine
Oh girl

Is there a way to find the cure for this implanted in a pill?
It's just the name upon the bottle which determines if it will
Is the problem you're allergic to a well familiar name?
Do you have a problem with this one if the results are the same?

Acetaminophen, you see the medicine

Oh girl, you have no faith in medicine
Oh girl, you have no faith in medicine
Acetaminophen, you see the medicine
Oh girl

Girl, you have no faith in medicine
Acetaminophen, you see the medicine
Oh girl

Well, strip the bark right off a tree and just hand it this way
Don't even need a drink of water to make that headache go away
Give me a sugar pill and watch me just rattle down the street

Acetaminophen, you see the medicine
Oh girl, you have no faith in medicine
Oh girl, you have no faith in medicine
Oh girl, oh girl, oh girl, oh girl

IT'S TRUE THAT WE LOVE ONE ANOTHER

Jack and Holly Golightly: Well, it's true that we love one another.
Holly: I love Jack White like a little brother.
Jack: Well, Holly, I love you too. But there's just so much that I don't know about you.

Holly: Jack, give me some money to pay my bills.
Jack: All the dough I give you, Holly, you've been using on pain pills.
Holly: Jack, will you call me if you're able?
Jack: I got your phone number written in the back of my Bible.

Holly: Jack, I think you're pulling my leg. And I think maybe I better ask Meg. Meg, do you think Jack really loves me?
Meg: You know I don't care cause Jack really bugs me. Why don't you ask him now?
Holly: Well, I would, but Meg, I really just don't know how.

Meg: Just say, "Jack , do you adore me?"
Jack: Well, I would, Holly, but love really bores me.
Jack and Holly: Then I guess we should just be friends.
Jack: I'm just kidding, Holly. Youu know that I'll love you 'til the end.

Jack and Holly: Well, it's true that we love one another.
Holly: I love Jack White like a little brother
Jack: Well, Holly, I love you too. But there's just so much that I don't know about you.

Jack: Holly, give me some of your English lovin.'
Holly: If I did that, Jack, I'd have one in the oven. Why don't you go off and love yourself?
Jack: If I did that, Holly, there won't be anything left for anybody else.
Holly: Jack it's too bad about the way that you look.
Jack: You know I gave that horse a carrot so he'd break your foot.
Meg: Will the two of you cut it out? And tell 'em what it's really all about.

Holly and Jack: Well, it's true that we love one another.
Holly: I love Jack White like a little brother.
Jack: Well, Holly, I love you too. But there's just so much that I don't know about you.

Get Behind Me Satan

1. BLUE ORCHID 149
2. THE NURSE 151
3. MY DOORBELL 153
4. FOREVER FOR HER (IS OVER FOR ME) 157
5. LITTLE GHOST 159
6. THE DENIAL TWIST 161
7. WHITE MOON 163
8. INSTINCT BLUES 165
9. PASSIVE MANIPULATION 167
10. TAKE, TAKE, TAKE 171
11. AS UGLY AS I SEEM 173
12. RED RAIN 175
13. I'M LONELY (BUT I AIN'T THAT LONELY YET) 177

BLUE ORCHID

You got a reaction
You got a reaction, didn't you?
You took a white orchid
You took a white orchid and turned it blue

Something better than nothing
Something better than nothing, it's giving up
We all need to do something
Try to keep the truth from showing up

How dare you
How old are you now, anyway?
How dare you
How old are you now, anyway?
How dare you
How old are you now, anyway?

You're given a flower
But I guess that there's just no pleasing you
Your lip tastes sour
But you think that it's just me teasing you

You got a reaction
You got a reaction, didn't you?
You took a white orchid
You took a white orchid and turned it blue

Get behind me
Get behind me now, anyway
Get behind me
Get behind me now, anyway
Get behind me
Get behind me now, anyway

You got a reaction

You got a reaction, didn't you?
You took a white orchid
You took a white orchid and turned it blue

THE NURSE

The nurse should not be the one who puts salt in your wounds
But it's always with trust that the poison is fed with a spoon
When you're helpless with no one to turn to alone in your room
You would swear that the one who would care for you never would leave
She promised and said, "You will always be safe here with me"
But promises open the door to be broken to me

No, I'm never, no, I'm never, no, I'm never gonna let you down now
No, I'm never, no, I'm never, no, I'm never gonna let you down
No, I'm never, no, I'm never, no, I'm never gonna let you down now
No, I'm never, no, I'm never, no, I'm never gonna let you down

The maid that you've hired could never conspire to kill
She's to mother, not quietly smother you when you're most ill
The one that you're trusting suspiciously dusting the sill

No, I'm never, no, I'm never, no, I'm never gonna let you down now
No, I'm never, no, I'm never, no, I'm never gonna let you down
No, I'm never, no, I'm never, no, I'm never gonna let you down now
No, I'm never, no, I'm never, no, I'm never gonna let you down

MY DOORBELL

I'm thinking about my doorbell
When ya gonna ring it, when you going to ring it
Yeah, I'm thinking about my doorbell
When ya gonna ring it, when you going to ring it
Yeah, I'm thinking about my doorbell
When ya gonna ring it, when you going to ring it
Yeah, I been thinking about my doorbell
Oh well

Well, women and children need kisses
Not the man in my life I know
And I been going to mystery misses
I respect the art of the show
Take back what you said, little girl
And while you're at it take yourself back too
Well, I'm tired of sitting here waiting
Woman, what you going to do now
What you going to do about it

I'm thinking about my doorbell
When ya gonna ring it, when you going to ring it
I'm thinking about my doorbell
When ya gonna ring it, when you going to ring it, oh
I'm thinking about my doorbell
When ya gonna ring it, when you going to ring it
Yeah, I been thinking about my doorbell
Oh well

You don't seem to come around
Point your finger and make a sound
You don't seem to come around
Knock knock since you knocked it down
Oh well
Make a sound and I'll make you feel right

Right at home, yeah
Yeah, right at home

Nobody got me waiting in pain
But how come it's so easy to you
You don't strike me as the type to be callous
But your words seem so obtuse
But then again I know you feel guilty
And you tell me you want me again
But I don't need any of your pity
I got plenty of my own friends
They're all above me

And I been thinking about my doorbell
When they gonna ring it, when they going to ring it
Yeah, I been thinking about my doorbell
When they gonna ring it, when they going to ring it
Oh, I been thinking about my doorbell
When they gonna ring it, when they going to ring it
Yeah, I been thinking about my doorbell
Oh well

They don't seem to come around
Push the finger and make a sound
They don't seem to come around
Maybe then they'll knock 'em down
Oh well

Make a sound and I'll make you feel right
Right at home
Right at home

I'm thinking about my doorbell
When ya gonna ring it, when you going to ring it
I'm thinking about my doorbell
When ya gonna ring it, when you going to ring it
I'm thinking about my doorbell
When ya gonna ring it, when you going to ring it
Yeah, I been thinking about my doorbell
When ya gonna ring it, when you going to ring it

Yeah, I'm thinking about my doorbell
When ya gonna ring it, when you going to ring it
Yeah, I'm thinking about my doorbell

Oh, oh well

FOREVER FOR HER (IS OVER FOR ME)

I blew it
And if I knew what to do, then I'd do it
But the point that I have, I'll get to it
And forever for her is over for me
Forever, just the word that she said that means never
To be with another together
And with the weight of a feather it tore into me
Then I knew it
All the work that it took to get through it
On the wings of a feather that flew it
Fell onto my shoe it cut up into me

Well, everybody's reaction is changing you
But their love is only a fraction of what I can give to you

So let's do it, just get on a plane and just do it
Like the birds and the bees and get to it
Just get out of town and forever be free
Forever, a word that we could say together
It could change if you want for the better
Just turn down my shirt and lay down next to me

I blew it
And if I knew what to do, then I'd do it
But the point that I have, I'll get to it
And forever for her is over for me
Forever, just the word that she said that means never
To be with another together
And with the weight of a feather it tore into me

Well, everybody's reaction is changing you
But their love is only a fraction of what I can give to you

Well, let's do it, just get on a plane and just do it
Like the birds and the bees and get to it

Just get out of town and forever be free
Forever, a word we could say together
It could change if you want for the better
Just turn down my shirt and lay down next to me

LITTLE GHOST

Little ghost, little ghost
One I'm scared of the most
Can you scare me up a little bit of love?
I'm the only one that sees you
And I can't do much to please you
And it's not yet time to meet the lord above

The first moment that I met her
I did not expect a specter
When I shook her hand I really shook a glove
She looked into me so sweetly
And we left the room discreetly
No one else could know the secret of our love

Little ghost, little ghost
One I'm scared of the most
Can you scare me up a little bit of love?
I'm the only one that sees you
And I can't do much to please you
And it's not yet time to meet the lord above

Every morning I awoke
And I see my little ghost
Wondering if it's really her that's lying there
I lean to touch her and I whisper
But not brave enough to kiss her
When I held her I was really holding air

Little ghost, little ghost
One I'm scared of the most
Can you scare me up a little bit of love?
I'm the only one that sees you
And I can't do much to please you
And it's not yet time to meet the lord above

Though I try my best to keep it
There really was no secret
Must have looked like I was dancing with the wall
No one else could see this apparition
But because of my condition
I fell in love with a little ghost and that was all

Little ghost, little ghost
One I'm scared of the most
Can you scare me up a little bit of love?
I'm the only one that sees you
And I can't do much to please you
And it's not yet time to meet the lord above
No, it's not your time to meet the lord above

THE DENIAL TWIST

If you think that a kiss is all in the lips
C'mon, you got it all wrong, man
And if you think that our dance was all in the hips
Oh well, then do the twist
If you think holding hands is all in the fingers
Grab hold of the soul where the memory lingers and
Make sure to never do it with the singer
Cause he'll tell everyone in the world
What he was thinking about the girl
Yeah, what he's thinking about the girl

A lot of people get confused and they bruise
Real easy when it comes to love
They start putting on their shoes and walking out
And singing "boy, I think I had enough"
Just because she makes a big rumpus
She don't mean to be mean or hurt you on purpose, boy
Take a tip and do yourself a little service
Take a mountain turn it into a mole
Just by playing a different role
Yeah, by playing a different role

The boat, yeah, you know she's rockin' it
And the truth, well, ya know there's no stoppin' it
The boat, yeah, you know she's still rockin' it
The truth, well, you know there's no stoppin' it

So what, somebody left you in a rut
And wants to be the one who's in control
But the feeling that you're under can really make you wonder
How the hell she can be so cold
So now you're mad, denying the truth
And it's hidden in the wisdom in the back of your tooth
Ya need to spit it out, in a telephone booth
While ya call everyone that you know, and ask 'em

Where do you think she goes
Oh yeah, where d'ya suppose she goes, oh

The truth, well, you know there's no stoppin' it
And the boat, well, yeah know she's still rockin' it
The boat, well, you know she's still rockin' it
And the truth, yeah, you know there's no stoppin' it

You recognize the effect and the wreck
That it's causin' when she rocks the boat
But it's the clause hidden in the Cardinal Laws
'bout the proper place to hang her coat
So to you, the truth is still hidden
And the soul plays the role of a lost little kitten but
You should know that the doctors weren't kiddin?
She's been singing it all along
But you were hearin' a different song
Yeah, you were hearin' a different song
But you were hearin' a different song

WHITE MOON

White moon, white moon
Breaks open the tune
Of a deserted cartoon that I wrote
Creature come, creature, creature
My own double-feature
As I'm warming the bleachers at home

Well, my nose keeps on bleeding
Cause it's Rita I'm needing
I better call out a meeting of the boys
Of the boys

My friends are all dying
And death can't be lying
It's the truth and it don't make a noise
Oh Rita, oh Rita
If you lived in Reseda
I would move you with the beat of a drum
And this picture is proof
That although you're aloof
You had the shiniest tooth 'neath the sun

Easy come, easy go
Be a star of the show
I'm giving up all I know to get more
To get more

Photograph the picture
Young grunt pin-up scripture
For the locker-tagged memories of war
A mirage, this garage
And a photo montage
And the finger massage from the host

Good Lord, good Lord
The one I adored
That I cannot afford is a ghost
Is a ghost

Proto-social is the word
And the word is the bird
That flew through the herd in the snow
In the snow

Lemonade me, then grade me
Then deliver my baby
And if my friends all persuade me, I'll go
Blink, blink at me Rita
Don't you know I'm a bleeder?
And I promised I wouldn't lead her on

But she read me, then led me
And I ate what was fed me
'Til I purged every word in this song

INSTINCT BLUES

Well, the crickets get it
And the ants get it
I bet you the pigs get it
Yeah, even the plants get it
Come on now, and get with it
Yeah, I want you to get with it
Yeah, I just want you to get with it

'Cause every worm that's under your shoe
And every bird and bug in the jungle, too
And everything in the ocean blue
They just happen to know exactly what to do
So why don't you?
Yeah, why don't you?

The flies get it
And the frogs get it
And all them big jungle cats get it
And I bet your little dog gets it
Yeah, I want you to get with it
Yeah, come on, and get with it
Yeah, I just want you to get with it

'Cause every worm that's under your shoe
And every bird and bee in the jungle, too
And everything in the ocean blue
They just happen to know exactly what to do
So why don't you?
Yeah, why don't you?

And all the chickens get it
And them singing canaries get it
Even strawberries get it
I want you to get with it
Yeah, I want you to get with it
Yeah, I just want you to get with it

'Cause every worm that's under your shoe
And every bird and bee in the jungle, too
And everything in the ocean blue
They just happen to know exactly what to do
So, why don't you?
Yeah, why don't you?

PASSIVE MANIPULATION

Women, listen to your mothers
Don't just succumb to the wishes of your brothers
Take a step back, take a look at one another
You need to know the difference
Between a father and a lover

TAKE, TAKE, TAKE

I was sitting there in a comfortable chair
And that was all that I needed
Then my friend offered me a drink for us to share
And that was all that I needed
Well, then I felt at ease but then I'm not too hard to please
I guess you couldn't call me greedy
Then I was shocked to look up and see Rita Hayworth there
In a place so seedy
She walked into the bar with her long, red, curly hair
And that was all that I needed
And I said to my friend, "good god, we're lucky men
Just to even see her"

Take, take, take
Take, take, take
Take, take, take

And I could not resist, I just had to get close to her
And that was all that I needed
I walked and loomed around her table for a while
And that was all that I needed
Then I said, "I hate to bug you, ma'am, but can I have your autograph?"
And that was all that I needed
She pressed her lips against a white piece of paper
And that was all that I needed
Then I saw what she wrote, "My heart is in my mouth"
And that was all that I needed
Then she handed it to me, and I think that she could see
That that was all that I needed
I started to walk away but then I remembered
"Hey, I forgot to get a picture"
So I asked her one more time, "Could I have another favor?"
That was all that I needed
She was kind and posed with me then I knew my friend would see
My celebrity meeting

Take, take, take
Take, take, take
Take, take, take

She turned and said to me, "I need to go to sleep,"
And it seemed so mean
It's almost as if she could not appreciate
How cool I was being
She said, "good night" and walked away and I didn't know what to say
I just couldn't believe it
Well, it's just not fair, I want to get a piece of hair
That was all that I needed
Or maybe a kiss on the cheek, I wouldn't wash it for a week
That would be all that I needed
But she didn't even care that I was even there
What a horrible feeling

AS UGLY AS I SEEM

I, I'm as ugly as I seem
Worse than all your dreams
Could ever make me out to be
And it makes me want to scream
When it's Halloween
And the kids are laughing
The rogue is a bank he's never broke
But worth as much as a joke that no one is laughing at

Can you believe some things are not
Appealing as a spot
On the ceiling of my childhood bedroom
And can these dreams that you can't imagine
Will never match the vision
That you had decided for me
You are to take away from me
Things that are mine and it's not your right
I bet you wouldn't expect a fight
Can it be that I don't want what you want?
And the only thing I could care for
Is a place in a home that is safe and warm
Safe and warm, safe and warm, safe and warm

Judge yourself if you feel the need
Just let me known to be
In search of the truth myself
There is a drop of blood on the ground
And it seems to me that it's not my kind
And I can't be sure if it's yours or mine

I am as ugly as I seem
Worse than all your dreams
Could ever make me
Could ever make me
Could ever make me
Could ever make me

RED RAIN

Can't you hear me?
Can't you hear me calling your name girl?

I'm standing, standing in the red, red rain
In the morning, standing in the red, red rain
Can't you hear me?
Can't you hear me calling your name, girl?
In the morning, when I'm standing in the red, red rain, girl
In the morning, I'm standing in the red, red rain
Can't you hear me?
Can't you hear me calling your name, girl?
In the morning, when I'm standing in the red, red rain, girl

You think not telling is the same as not lying, don't you?
Then I guess not feeling is the same as not crying to you
You think not telling is the same as not lying, don't you?
Then I guess not feeling is the same as not crying to you

In the red, in the rain, in the rain
In the red, in the red, in the rain, in the rain
In the red, in the red, in the rain, in the rain
In the red, in the red, in the rain, in the rain

If there is a lie, then there is a liar too
And if there is a sin, then there is a sinner too
And If there is a lie, then there is a liar too
And if there is a sin, then there is a sinner too

In the red, in the red, in the rain, in the rain
On the red, On the red, in the rain, in the rain
In the red, in the red, in the rain, in the rain
On the red, on the red, in the rain, in the rain
In the red, in the red, in the rain, in the rain

Can't you hear me?
Can't you hear me calling your name, girl?

I'M LONELY (BUT I AIN'T THAT LONELY YET)

Well, I miss my mother
And I miss being her son
As crazy as I was I
Guess I wasn't much of one
Sometimes I miss her so much
I want to hop on the next jet
And I get lonely, but I ain't that lonely yet

And I love my sister
Lord knows how I've missed her
She loves me
And she knows I won't forget
And sometimes I get jealous
Of all her little pets
And I get lonely, but I ain't that lonely yet

I roll over in bed
Looking for someone to touch
There's a girl that I know of
But don't ask for much
She's homely, and she's cranky
And her hair's in a net
And I'm lonely, but I ain't that lonely yet

Are you my friend when I need one
I need someone to be one
I take anybody I can get
And sometimes I wanna call you
And I feel like a pest
And I'm lonely, but I ain't that lonely yet

I went down to the river
Filled with regret
I looked down and I wondered
If there was any reason left

I left just before my lungs could get wet
I'm lonely, but I ain't that lonely yet

And I love my sister
Lord knows how I've missed her
She loves me
And she knows I won't forget
And sometimes I get jealous
Of all her little pets
And I get lonely, but I ain't that lonely yet
Yeah I get lonely, but I ain't that lonely yet

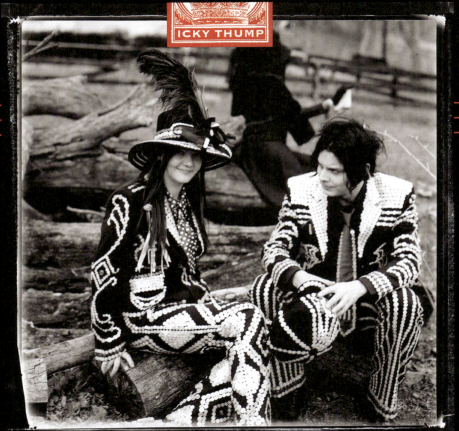

Icky Thump

1. ICKY THUMP 183

2. YOU DON'T KNOW WHAT LOVE IS (YOU JUST DO WHAT YOU'RE TOLD) 185

3. 300 M.P.H. TORRENTIAL OUTPOUR BLUES 187

4. CONQUEST (written by Corky Robbins)

5. BONE BROKE 189

6. PRICKLY THORN, BUT SWEETLY WORN 191

7. ST. ANDREW (THIS BATTLE IS IN THE AIR) 193

8. LITTLE CREAM SODA 197

9. RAG AND BONE 199

10. I'M SLOWLY TURNING INTO YOU 203

11. A MARTYR FOR MY LOVE FOR YOU 205

12. CATCH HELL BLUES 207

13. EFFECT AND CAUSE 209

ICKY THUMP

IIIIIIIIEEEEEEE
Icky thump
Who'da thunk?
Sittin' drunk on a wagon to Mexico
What a chump
Well, my head got a bump
When I hit it on the radio
Redhead señorita
Lookin' dead
Came and said,
"Need a bed?" en Español
I said, "Gimme a drink of water
I'm gonna sing around the collar
And I don't need a microphone"

Icky thump
With a lump in my throat
Grabbed my coat
And I was freaking
I was ready to go
And I swear besides the hair
She had one white eye
One blank stare
Lookin' up, lyin' there
On the stand near her hand
Was a candy cane
Black rum, sugar cane
Dry ice, (and) something strange
La La La La La La La
La La La La La La La

White Americans
What, nothing better to do?
Why don't you kick yourself out?
You're an immigrant too

Who's usin' who?
What should we do?
Well, you can't be a pimp
And a prostitute too
Icky thump
Handcuffed to a bunk
Robbed blind
Looked around
And there was nobody else
Left alone, I hit myself with a stone
Went home
And learned how to clean up after myself

YOU DON'T KNOW WHAT LOVE IS
(YOU JUST DO WHAT YOU'RE TOLD)

In some respects
I suspect you've got a respectable side
When pushed and pulled and pressured
You seldom run and hide
But it's for someone else's benefit
Not for what you wanna do
Until I realize that you've realized
I'm gonna say these words to you

You don't know what love is
You do as you're told
Just as a child at ten might act
But you're far too old
You're not hopeless or helpless
And I hate to sound cold
But you don't know what love is
You just do as you're told

I can see your man
Can't help but win
Any problems that may arise
But in his mind there can be no sin
If you never criticize
You just keep on repeating
All those empty "I love you's"
Until you say you deserve better
I'm gonna lay right into you

You don't know what love is
You just do as you're told
Just as a child of ten might act
But you're far too old
Your not hopeless or helpless
And I hate to sound cold
But you don't know what love is

No, you don't know what love is
No, you don't know what love is
You just do as you're told
Yeah, do as you're told

300 M.P.H. TORRENTIAL OUTPOUR BLUES

I'm bringing back ghosts
That are no longer there
I'm getting hard on myself
Sitting in my easy chair
Well, there's three people in the mirror
And I'm wondering which one of them I should choose
Well, I can't keep from laughing
Spitting out these 300 mile per hour outpour blues

I'm breaking my teeth off
Trying to bite my lip
There's all kinds of red-headed women
That I ain't supposed to kiss
And it's that color which never fails
To turn me blue
So I just swallow it and hold on to it
And use it to scare the hell out of you

I have a woman
Says, "Come and watch me bleed"
And I'm wondering just how I can do that
And still give her everything that she needs
Well, there's three people in my head that have the answer
And one of them has got to be you
But you're holding tight to it, the answer
Singing these 300 mile per hour outpour blues

Put on gloves, a tied scarf and wrap up warm
On this winter night
Every time you get defensive
You're just looking for a fight
It's safe to sing somebody out there's got a problem
With almost anything you'll do
Well, next time they stab you don't fight back just play the victim
Instead of playing the fool

And the roads are covered with a million
Little molecules
Of cigarette ashes and the school floors are covered
With pieces of pencil eraser too
Well, sooner or later the ground's gonna be holding all
Of my ashes too
But I can't help but wonder if after I'm gone will I still have these 300 mile
per hour, finger breaking, no answers making, battered dirty hands, bee
stung and busted up, empty cup torrential outpour blues

One thing's for sure: in that graveyard
I'm gonna have the shiniest pair of shoes

BONE BROKE

Look closer and you can see how I been running it
I got a dollar bill in the cockpit
Surprised being white is a black hole?
I got another job at the liquor store, damn
Oh well, I'm bone broke

They got a white pony in the stable
And ride him when the doggie isn't able
But he don't really care because they pay him
But still a black suit is going to shake him down
Oh well, I'm bone broke
Yeah, broke as I'll ever be

Look another way girl, I'm telling ya
God gave seven minutes right to ya
And your mother put her money into platinum
And now you never have to pay attention
Do ya? Do ya?

I'm leaning on a brick with my nails
I'm sending in the money's in the mail
Keep showing that my bones never fake it
But now the brick bank is gonna break it down
Oh well, I'm bone broke

Look another way girl I'm telling ya
God gave seven minutes right to ya
Your mother put her money into platinum
So that you wouldn't have to pay attention

PRICKLY THORN, BUT SWEETLY WORN

Singing
Li de li de li, oh, oh
Well, a li de li de li, oh
Li de li de li, oh, oh, oh
Well, a li de li de li, oh

Well, the hills are pretty and rollin'
But the thorn is sharp and swollen
And the man plays a beautiful whistle
But he wears a prickly thistle

Singing
Li de li de li, oh, oh, oh
Well, a li de li de li, oh
Li de li de li, oh, oh, oh
Well, a li de li de li, oh

The silver birches pierce through an icy fog
Which covers the ground most daily
And the angels which carry St. Andrew high
Are singing a tune most gaily

Singing
Li de li de li, oh, oh
Well, a li de li de li, oh
Li de li de li, oh, oh
Well, a li de li de li, oh

One sound can hold back a thousand hands
When the pipe blows a tune forlorn
And the thistle is a prickly flower
Aye, but how it is sweetly worn

Singing
Li de li de li, oh, oh
Well, a li de li de li, oh
Li de li de li, oh, oh, oh
Well, a li de li de li, oh
Li de li de li, oh, oh
Well, a li de li de li, oh
Li de li de li, oh, oh
Well, a li de li de li, oh

ST. ANDREW (THIS BATTLE IS IN THE AIR)

This battle is in the air
I'm looking upwards
Where are the angels?
I'm not in my home
St. Andrew don't forsake me
St. Andrew?
Don't forsake me
Who is here to greet me?
The children are crying
I'm not in my home
I travel backwards in ecstasy
Where are the angels?
Don't forget me
St. Andrew
I've been true
What do I need to say?
What do I need to say?
The children are crying

LITTLE CREAM SODA

One, two, three, four

Well, every highway that I go down
Seems to be longer than the last one that I knew about
Oh well
And every girl that I walk around
Seems to be more of an illusion than the last one I found
Oh well
And this old man in front of me wearing canes and ruby rings
It's like containing an explosion when he sings
And with every chance to set himself on fire
He just ends up doing the same thing

Well, each beautiful thing I come across
Tells me to stop moving and shake this riddle off
Oh well
And there was a time when all I wanted
Was my ice cream colder and a little cream soda
Oh well, oh well
And a wooden box and an alley full of rocks
Was all I had to care about
Oh well, oh well, oh well

Now my mind is filled with rubber tires and forest fires
And whether I'm a liar
And lots of other situations
Where I don't know what to do
At which time God screams to me,
"There's nothing left for me to tell you"
Nothing left for me to tell you
Nothing left

Oh well, oh well, oh well, oh well
Oh well, oh well, oh well, oh well

RAG AND BONE

Jack: Mmm...
Meg: Rag and bone
Jack: Rag and bone
Meg: Rag and bone
Jack: Rag-a-bone
Meg, look at this place
Meg: What? Ooh...
Jack: Well, this place is like a mansion. It's like a mansion, look at all this stuff
Meg: I don't know...
Jack: Look, I see something over there
Meg: Ooh...
Jack: Man

Well,
Can't you hear us yelling "rag and bone"?
Bring out your junk
And we'll give it a home
A broken trumpet
Or a telephone
A c'mon, a c'mon, a c'mon
C'mon and give it to me

A c'mon, a c'mon, a c'mon
C'mon and give it to me
Rag and bone, rag and bone
A c'mon, a c'mon, a c'mon
C'mon and give it to me

All of your pretty, your pretty little rags and bones

Jack: Well, man, look at all this, you don't want it?
Meg: Mmm. Ooh. I can use that
Jack: You sure you don't want it, man? I can use...
Meg: Mmm-hmm
Jack: Take it. It's just things that you don't want I can use 'em. Meg can use 'em

Meg: Mmm-hmm
Jack: We can do something with 'em. We'll make something out of 'em
Meg: Mmm-hmm
Jack: Make some money out of 'em at least
Meg: Mmm-hmm. This fits me perfect. Give it to me
Jack: Hey, if you ain't gonna use it, just give it to us. We'll give it a home

Have you got something shiny for me?
Anybody got a Christmas tree?
Can you part with a toilet seat?
A jump up, a jump up, a jump up
C'mon and give it to me
Rag and bone

We wanna get it, granny
While it's hot
You think it's trash, granny
But it's not
A we'll be taking
Whatever you got
A give up, a give up, a give up
Come on and give it to me

All of your pretty, your pretty little rags and bones

Meg: I saw some stuff in your yard, are you going to give it to us...
Jack: Aw, Meg, don't be rude
Meg: ...or not?
Jack: They might need it. If you don't want it, we'll take it. If you don't
want to give it to us, we keep walking by. We keep going, we're not tired,
but got plenty of places to go, lots of home we ain't been to yet. On
the west side, the southwest side, Middle East, rich house, dog house,
outhouse, old folks house. House for unwed mothers, halfway homes,
catacombs, twilight zones. Looking for Technics turntables to gramo-
phones. So take a last lick of your ice cream cone, and lock up what you
still want to own. But please be kind...
Meg: Take your time
Jack: ...and don't rewind
Meg: That's fine
Jack: All of your pretty

Your pretty little rags and bones
Your pretty little rags and bones

A jump up, a jump up, a jump up
C'mon and give it to me
Ah, ah, oh, your pretty little rags and bones
Jack and Meg: A c'mon, a c'mon, a c'mon
C'mon and give it to us

I'M SLOWLY TURNING INTO YOU

I'm slowly turning into you
But you don't know this
To be true
You say I'm lying and I never really tell you the truth
But your face is getting older
So put your head on my shoulder
Yeah, put your head on my shoulder

Yesterday it hit me that I do all the little things
That you do
Except the same little things that you do are annoying
They're annoying as hell in fact
It kinda struck a little bell in fact
I like to keep my little shell intact

And I'm slowly turning into you
And I'm slowly turning into you

Then something else came to mind
That was the mirror
It made everything clearer
That you're more beautiful, compelling and stronger
It didn't take much longer
Just for me to realize I love all the little things
And the beauty that they're gonna bring
I dig your little laugh and I'm lovin' your quick wit
I even love it when you're faking it
And it might sound a little strange for me to say to you
But I'm proud to be you

And I'm slowly turning into you
And I'm slowly turning into you
And I'm slowly turning into you
And I'm slowly turning into you

A MARTYR FOR MY LOVE FOR YOU

She was sixteen and six feet tall
In a crowd of teenagers coming out of the zoo
She stumbled, started to slip and fall
Teeter-tottered on the top of patent leather shoes
I happened to catch her and said
"Maybe these ruby shoes are a little cumbersome for you"
Maybe for you, now

But not as shaky as I must have seemed
Talking junk through her giggle, little teenage dream
And on the phone I could not compete
My dumb-luck fake confidence was getting weak
For a sec' I thought I sounded sweet
But sure enough in a gruff, faint voice
I heard myself speak

I could stay a while
But sooner or later, I'll break your smile
And I can tell a joke
But one of these days I'm bound to choke
And we could share a kiss
But I feel like I can't go through with this
And I bet we could build a home
But I know the right thing for me to do
Is to leave you alone
Leave you alone, now

I'm beginning to like you
So you probably won't get what I'm going to do
I'm walking away from you
It probably don't make much sense to you
But I'm trying to save you
From all of the things that I'll probably say or do
I'll probably do

I could stay a while
But sooner or later, I'll break your smile
And I can tell a joke
But one of these days I'm bound to choke
And we might share a kiss
But I feel like I can't go through with this
And I bet we could build a home
But I know the right thing for me to do
Is to leave you alone
Leave you alone, now

You'll probably call me a fool
And say I'm doing exactly what a coward would do
And I'm beginning to like you
It's a shame, what a lame way to live
But what can I do?
I hope you appreciate what I do

I'm a martyr for my love for you
A martyr for my love for you, now
A martyr for my love for you
A martyr for my love for you

CATCH HELL BLUES

If you go looking for hot water—don't act shocked when you get—
burned a little bit
If you really want some hot water—I can help you find it

Well, if they catch me around, you're playing 'rock the boat'
I'm gonna catch hell
And if you're throwing your voice
In bed singing a note
I'm gonna catch hell
I know it
Yes, sir
Try and catch me
Wha'

Tricky, tricky
Yeah

If you're getting tricky, lying to yourself
You're gonna catch hell
And if you're testing God, lying to his face
You're gonna catch hell
Come on
Hey
That's it
They're gonna catch you
Huh-ho, they're gonna catch you

Easy

EFFECT AND CAUSE

I guess you have to have a problem
If you want to invent a contraption
First you cause a train wreck
Then they put me in traction
Well, first came an action
And then a reaction
But you can't switch 'em 'round
For your own satisfaction
Well, you burnt my house down
Then got mad
At my reaction
Well, in every complicated situation
Of a human relation
Makin' sense of it all
Takes a whole lotta concentration, mmm
Well, you can't blame a baby
For her pregnant ma
And if there's one of these unavoidable laws
It's that you just can't take the effect
And make it the cause, no

Well, you can't take the effect
And make it the cause
I didn't rob a bank
Because you made up the law
Blame me for robbin' Peter
But don't you blame Paul
Can't take the effect
And make it the cause

I ain't the reason that you gave me
No reason to return your call
You built a house of cards
And got shocked when you saw them fall
Well, I ain't saying I'm innocent

In fact the reverse
But if you're headed to the grave
You don't blame the hearse
You're like a little girl yellin' at her brother
'Cause you lost his ball
Well, you keep blaming me
For what you did
But that ain't all
The way you clean up a wreck
Is enough to give one pause, yes
Well, you seem to forget just how this song started
I'm reactin' to you
Because you left me brokenhearted
See you just can't just take the effect
And make it the cause

Well, you can't take the effect
And make it the cause
I didn't rob a bank
Because you made up the law
Blame me for robbin' Peter
But don't you blame Paul
Can't take the effect
And make it the cause

Songs from Singles, Compilations, and More

1. LET'S SHAKE HANDS 215
2. LAFAYETTE BLUES 217
3. CANDY CANE CHILDREN 219
4. RED BOWLING BALL RUTH 221
5. HAND SPRINGS 225
6. RED DEATH AT 6:14 227
7. THOUGH I HEAR YOU CALLING, I WILL NOT ANSWER 229
8. WHO'S A BIG BABY? 231
9. TOP SPECIAL 233
10. IT'S MY FAULT FOR BEING FAMOUS 235
11. CASH GRAB COMPLICATIONS ON THE MATTER 237
12. HONEY, WE CAN'T AFFORD TO LOOK THIS CHEAP 239
13. CITY LIGHTS 241

LET'S SHAKE HANDS

Oh, let's shake hands
Oh, baby, let's shake hands
Well, there's something here in the air
Jump up and let me know when you're there
Baby, let's shake hands
Oh, let's be friends
Oh, baby, let's be friends
I can't come up with a better plan
Put your fingers in my hand
Baby, let's be friends
Oh, say my name
Oh, baby, say my name
Well, you can do what you want to do
Throw it in the garbage can
But just say my name

LAFAYETTE BLUES

Mar-an-tette, Leverette
Lannette, Lafayette, Livernois
Labrosse, Louis, Mettetal
Rochelle, Marseilles
Riopelle, Manistique, Armour
Mercier, Lemay
Tournier, Saliotte et Leroy
Montlieu, Cadieux
Neveaux, Avenue en Detroit
Well, I'm ready
I'm ready
I'm ready, ready, ready to
Rock and roll
Lamphere, Belle Terre
Marseilles, Mettetal, et
Rouge, Le Blanc

CANDY CANE CHILDREN

Why don't you open me up?

Candy cane girl
Don't you know your name, girl?
Twelve people going to ask you just the same, girl
What a world
Christmas once again, girl
That's three hundred and sixty four tears, girl

So when Christmas finally comes
And nobody's got a gun
And you think it might be fun
To hang around
Think again, girl

Why don't you open me up?

Candy cane boy
Don't you know your name, boy?
Nine people going to tell you just the same, boy
You're a lone son
In the middle of a million
And nobody knows how to talk to children

Oh, when Christmas finally comes
And nobody's got a gun
And you think it might be fun
To get a new toy
Think again, boy

Oh, when Christmas finally comes
And no one's got a gun
And you think it might be fun
To make a stand
Think again, man

RED BOWLING BALL RUTH

Well, pay attention
Attention to my words
I love ya
I don't know what you heard
And this fellow
Has got to go for sure

Red bowling ball
Red bowling ball Ruth
Well, that's somethin'
That makes you know the truth
I set it rolling
And then it breaks your tooth

Well, Peter
Are you in the wrong town?
Well, I love this girl
So don't you come around?
And you leavin'
Will be the only sound

HAND SPRINGS

I took my girl to go bowling downtown at the Red Door
After an argument, I started because I thought she didn't like me anymore
I can't help it, sometimes I feel pitiful
And of course, she's so young and beautiful

I bought us two glasses of Coke
That's her favorite, and I wanted to make up for earlier
But I dropped her glass and it broke
So I just gave my glass to her

She laughed and so did I in our lane
Then she went to the vending machine to buy a candy cane
But right next to that was a boy I knew with a spring in his hand
Playing a country pinball machine called "Stand By Your Man"
I saw him talk to her, but I stayed in my lane and played my game steady
And was thinking of the day when i'd be too old to throw a ball this heavy

But I guess I'm young now, so it's easy to knock 'em all down
Then I looked and saw her say to him, "you're really hitting that ball around"
And he's looking at her the way I did when i first met her
I could see in his face white flowers and cups of coffee and love letters

I was sorry to interrupt that game
But I went and did it anyway
I dropped my red bowling ball through the glass of his machine
And said, "Are you quick enough to hit this ball, Mr. Clean?"
I was scared to lose her, so I couldn't help being mean

And that ended both of our games
I said I was sorry, but my girl left with him just the same
I thought how much I hate when love makes me act this way
I was bent over a broken pinball machine in a bowling alley and I threw
it all away
Well, isn't it all just a big game?

RED DEATH AT 6:14

(I'll buy it out there
Got a cop down at
6:14, 6:14?)

La la la la la la la la la la la la
La la la la la la
Whoo
What's that she said?
What's that she said
What's that she said
With her fingers turning blue
And her face was turning red
Whoo
Was that her dad?
Was that her dad
Was that her dad
With the magic marker
Writing little angel on her head

La la la la la la la la la la la la
La la la la la la la la la la la la

Whoo
She must be dead?
Well, she must be dead
She must be dead
If the only sound I hear
Are the devils by her bed

Whoo
What's that she said?
What's that she said
What's that she said
With her fingers turning blue
And her face was turning red
La la la la la la

THOUGH I HEAR YOU CALLING, I WILL NOT ANSWER

Though I hear you calling, I will not answer
Though I hear you calling, I will not answer

And the sun may shine right through your tooth, dear
And the wind may blow right through my ear

Though I hear you calling, I will not answer
Oh, I hear you calling, no I will not answer

And I broke your cold
And I broke your cold

Come on hit me…
…I will not answer, yeah
Though I hear you calling, no I will not answer

The sun may shine out to your mouth, dear
And the wind may blow right through my ear

Though I hear you calling, oh, I will not answer
Though I hear you calling, but I will not answer

Calling… and I broke your cold
I will not answer

Though I hear you calling, I will not answer
Though I hear you calling, but I will not answer
And I will not answer and I broke your cold
Uhmmm…Broke your cold
Yeah…uhmmm
Though I hear you calling... And the sun is shining
I will not answer... Right through your tooth, dear

WHO'S A BIG BABY?

Who's a big baby?
Who's a big baby?
Who's a big baby?
Waaahhhh
Who's a big baby?
Who's a big baby?
Who's a big baby?
Wah wah wah
Wah wah wah
Who's a big baby?
Who's a big baby?
Wahhhhhhhh
Wahhhhhhhh
Wah wah wah
Wah wah wah (shhh)
Who's a big baby?
Who's it?
Who's it?
Who's it?
Who's a big baby?
I want my mommy
Mommy
I want my mommy
Wahhhh
Who's a big baby?
Let's go shopping
Ladda ladda
Wahhhh
Ladda ladda ladda ladda ladda ladda ladda ladda ladda ladda ladda
ladda ladda ladda ladda
Who's a big baby?
Wahhhhhh wahhhhh wahhhhhhh wahhhhhhhh
Wahhhh wahhh wahhhhhhhh wahhhhhhh

TOP SPECIAL

Top special, baby!
Top! Top!
Top special!
Top special, baby!
You're my best friend!
Top! Top!
Top special!
Let's not fight, okay? Oh yeah.
Top special, baby!
Top! Top!
Top special!
It's cool, it's cool to go to school, it's cool!
Top special, baby!
Top! Top!
Top special!
All right, best friends til' the end, yeah!
Top special, baby!
Top! Top!

If I don't go to school, I don't get to see you...
...and that's not cool.
You're my best friend!

All right. Everybody keep it cool. Yeah. Let's keep it cool. Let's be friends.
Top special, baby!
Top! Top!
Top special!
Oh yeah!
Top special, baby! Oh! Yeah! Top!
Top special!
What? Why would you say something like that? But you're my best friend!
Wha? Uh... I don't understand...
It's not cool! It's not cool! It's not cool!
Come on. We can still be friends. No, we can still be friends! I mean it!
I don't want to be friends with her. I... I don't want to be friends with

him either. No. Okay. Here we go. No. Everythings cool. And then we're gonna go to get an ice cream after school and then together and I'll carry your books, then when we're on the bus I'm gonna play with you... I'm gonna play. You're still my top special friend, and we're gonna sit together on the bus... and um...

IT'S MY FAULT FOR BEING FAMOUS

She stuck a cellphone camera right into my face
With a flick of my wrist, I filled her nose full of mace
The cops want to know what was wrong with me
Didn't give me a chance to explain it, see?

It ain't her fault for being careless
It ain't her fault for being brainless
It ain't her fault for being hopeless
But it's my fault for being famous

I'm at the LAX, just checking my bag
When up comes a little paparazzi scumbag
I took a laptop, slapped him upside his head
The cops want to know why I left him for dead

It ain't his fault for being nameless
It ain't his fault for being thoughtless
It ain't his fault for being shameless
But it's my fault for being famous

I had a sweet old lady walk up to me
Wanted to get a photograph for her grandson to see
And as the digital camera lit up the place
She unloaded a chrome .45 in my face

But it ain't her fault for being ruthless
Ain't her fault for being toothless
Ain't her fault for being blameless
But it's my fault for being famous

CASH GRAB COMPLICATIONS ON THE MATTER

You tiptoed to me
As naked as a bone
Beautiful and canvas-blank, lily-white now
And just lookin' for a home
Yeah, and without trying to praise you
Well, I feel like I could raise you as my own

There's a duty to this loneliness
The good of everyone involved
And you're blind to my homeliness
One less mystery to solve
And the rest will be explained to you
As our bodies begin to revolve

What gave me this power to construct you?
Your guess is as good as mine
If you'd like me to return you to the stones from which I brought you
Well, you'll have to do your time

But for now, put down the gun
Start having fun
Forget the sun turning
And it will keep burning
As you melt into my mind

HONEY, WE CAN'T AFFORD TO LOOK THIS CHEAP

One, two, three

Well, I want to try and hold my head up high
In this busted-up Pinto truck conversion between the broken concrete and the cloudy sky
Well, you have to make an effort with me
Can you make it look like you're chauffeuring me?
There's enough gas to get us home now if we glide
When we took this job I thought that you knew the deal
I told the boss we had a Mercedes-Benz but all we got in our yard is a steering wheel
Well, I can't borrow this tuxedo much longer
Well, we might have to cut and sell your long hair
I don't mind you wearing a wig but I won't steal

Well, honey, we can't afford to look this cheap

We need to make it look like we're high class, so with a hollow cell phone, we can't be beat
I can't help but wonder, this time next year, will we be drinking Dom Perignon or reheated beer?

Well, honey, we can't afford to look this cheap

We have to keep up appearances as long as we can
There's too much to lose, our social status, well, our ice machine, and our ceiling fan
And if they find out that we ain't real songwriters
That we go Dutch on cigarette lighters
We're going to lose the paradise that's in our hands

Well, honey, we can't afford to look this cheap

Got an image to live up to here
In the best motel on Imposter Street

While the Joneses are waltzing off to dinner
We're gluing old lottery tickets together
Trying to make us a winner
Well, honey, we can't afford to look this cheap

CITY LIGHTS

I want to grab a stranger's hand and
Hold it as tightly as I can and
I will tell by their reaction if
They're like me or if I am crazy
When the lights of the city hit my
Eyes on the plane looking out the window
I am consumed by a comforting notion
That you are there and
I am welcome
If our miles have added up to
A giant pile of distance that we
Cannot reach past, climb, or conquer
Will you dig a
Tunnel to me?

Every move suspends an action
Any attempt to engage will push away
What you want becomes a magnet
Opposing poles
Never meeting
Can you combine a friend and mother?
Can you blend a dad and brother?
Must we have to pick one or the other?
Will we know this or always wonder?
Always wonder
You can tell what you've done to me
To be seen in hell from your place in a tree
Always helping
Ever loving
But will you always
Be above me

I won't ignore nor will not forget
The kindness that's been done to me
You are the surest and safest bet that

I could ask for
So I'm asking
Soon we will be side by side the
Plane will land and the wings will glide
The bags in hand and
The car will drive
Into you
I will arrive
By your side

III

ROUGH DRAFTS & EPHEMERA

✱ WELL IT'S TRUE THAT WE LOVE ONE ANOTHER
(H) I LOVE JACK WHITE LIKE A LITTLE BROTHER
③ WELL HOLLY I LOVE YOU TOO
③ BUT THERE'S JUST SO MUCH THAT I DON'T KNOW
ABOUT YOU.

(H) JACK GIVE ME SOME MONEY TO PAY MY BILLS
③ ALL THE DOUGH I GIVE YOU HOLLY YOU BEEN
USING ON PAIN PILLS ①   FAST

(H) JACK WILL YOU CALL ME IF YOUR ABLE? (D)
③ I GOT YOUR PHONE NUMBER WRITTEN IN THE BACK
OF MY BIBLE. (E)

(H) JACK I THINK YOU'RE PULLIN MY LEG (D)
(H) I THINK MAYBE I BETTER ASK MEG (A)
(H) MEG DO YOU THINK ~~JACK~~ JACK REALLY LOVES ME
(M) YOU KNOW I DON'T CARE CAUSE JACK REALLY BUGS ME.
(M) WHY DON'T YOU ASK HIM NOW?
(H) WELL I WOULD BUT MEG I REALLY JUST DON'T KNOW HOW.
(M) JUST SAY ~~~~ JACK ~~~~ ~~DO~~ YOU ADORE ME?
③ WELL I WOULD HOLLY EXCEPT LOVE REALLY BORES ME
✱ THEN I GUESS WE SHOULD JUST BE FRIENDS
③ IM JUST KIDDING HOLLY YOU KNOW THAT I'LL
LOVE YOU TILL THE END.
(CHORUS)

Pages 248-249: Handwritten, studio-used lyrics for "It's True that We Love One Another" complete with "J" and "M" and "H" designations for lines to be sung by Jack, Meg, and Holly Golightly.

(S) HOLLY GIVE ME SOME OF YOUR ENGLISH LOVIN
(H) IF I DID THAT JACK I'D HAVE ONE IN THE OVEN

(H) WHY DON'T YOU GO OFF AND LOVE YOURSELF
(S) IF I DID THAT HOLLY There won't be anything LEFT FOR ANY BODY ELSE

(H) JACK IT'S TOO BAD ABOUT THE WAY YOU LOOK
(S) YOU KNOW I GAVE THAT HORSE A RACE SO HE'D BREAK YOUR FOOT
(M) WILL THE TWO OF YOU CUT IT OUT.
(M) AND TELL THEM WHAT IT'S REALLY ALL ABOUT

(CHORUS)

1) I WANT TO HYPNOTIZE YOU BABY ON THE TELEPHONE
SO MANY TIMES IVE CALLED YOUR HOUSE JUST TO HEAR THE TONE,
AND THOUGH I KNEW THAT YOU WEREN'T HOME
I DIDN'T MIND TOO MUCH CAUSE IM SO ALONE.
I WANT TO HYPNOTIZE YOU BABY ON THE TELEPHONE.

3) I WANT TO HOLD YOUR LITTLE HAND IF I CAN BE SO BOLD
AND BE YOUR RIGHT HAND MAN TILL YOUR HANDS GET OLD
AND WHEN ALL THE FEELINGS GONE
JUST DECIDE IF YOU WANT TO KEEP HOLDING ON.
I WANT TO HOLD YOUR LITTLE HAND IF I CAN BE SO BOLD
I WANT TO TRY TO UNDERSTAND WHY YOU LIVE AT ALL
AND WHY YOU TREAT ME SO BAD WHEN I TRY TO CALL
YOU MAKE ME FEEL LIKE IM 3 FEET TALL
AND YOUR LACK OF CONCERN MAKES ME PUNCH THE WALL

2) I WANNA KEEP DRIVING THRU TILL I SEE YOUR EYES
YOURE THE KIND OF GIRL A GUY LIKE ME COULD HYPNOTIZE
AND IF THIS COMES AS A SURPRISE
JUST THINK OF ALL THE GUYS
WHO WOULD TELL YOU LIES

1-7-99

Handwritten lyrics to "Hypnotize" with alternate lines.

① PATIENT OF THIS PLAN
AND HUMBLE AS I CAN
IM ~~LEARNING~~ EVERY DAY
YOUR SHOWING ME THE WAY
BUT KNOW THIS MUCH IS TRUE
NO MATTER WHAT I DO
OFFEND IN EVERY WAY
SO TELL ME WHAT TO SAY

WEDNESDAY
A ~~EMPTY~~ FUNERAL
② ~~A FUNERAL THE~~
THE ~~COMPANYS~~ FULL
I GUESS ~~YOURE~~ ALONE TO SEE
WHOS BETTER YOU OR ME
AND ~~THINKING ALL ALONE~~
~~DISPLAYING EVERY TUNE~~

IM CARVING OUT A HOME
NO MATTER HOW ALONE
- SHOWING ALL MISTAKES
DISPLAYING EVERY TUNE

② THIS WEDNESDAY FUNERAL
THE BOULEVARD IS FULL
~~AND~~
~~MUST BE HARD TO HEAR~~ ME SAY
BE HAPPY ANYWAY
AS IM CARVING OUT A HOME
NO MATTER HOW ALONE
SHOWING ALL MY YOUTH
DISPLAYING EVERY TUNE

Pages 251-253: Working draft of "Offend in Every Way."

(1) PATIENT OF THIS PLAN
AND HUMBLE AS I CAN
~~strikethrough~~   COUNTING EVERY ~~EYE~~
~~strikethrough~~   TILL THOUDAY I DIE

~~strikethrough~~ KNOW THIS MUCH IS TRUE
NO MATTER WHAT I DO
OFFEND IN EVERY WAY
SO TELL ME WHAT O SAY

(2) THIS TUESDAY FUNERAL
THE BOULEVARD IS FULL   A FAKE
ITS HARD TO ~~KNOW TELL~~
~~strikethrough~~ ~~ITS~~ ~~strikethrough~~   ITS HARD TO STAY
~~I THINK~~   AWAKE
~~strikethrough~~ OF HOW WE LOOK
ITS RIGHT OUT OF A BOOK
~~THE TRUTH IS NOT THE WAY~~
~~strikethrough~~
TILL ~~ME THIS IS OUR~~ DAY
OFFEND IN EVERY WAY

(3) IM CARVING OUT A HOME
NO MATTER HOW ALONE
SHOWING ALL MY YOUTH
ITS BURNING FROM THE TRUTH
                      TIME
IM WAITING FOR THE ~~strikethrough~~
~~strikethrough~~
ALTHOUGH THEY LET ME STAY
OFFEND IN EVERY WAY

1. IM CARVING OUT A HOME
NO MATTER HOW ALONE
SHOWING ALL MY YOUTH
ITS BURNING FROM THE TRUTH
IM WAITING FOR THE TIME
WHEN NOONE ELSE'LL MIND
ALTHOUGH THEY LET ME STAY
OFFEND IN EVERY WAY

2. THIS TUESDAY FUNERAL
THE BOULEVARD IS FULL
ITS HARD TO TELL A FAKE
ITS HARD TO STAY AWAKE
I THINK OF HOW WE LOOK
ITS RIGHT OUT OF A BOOK
TILL THIS IS OUR DAY
OFFEND IN EVERY WAY

3. PATIENT OF THIS PLAN
AND HUMBLE AS I CAN
COUNTING EVERY EYE
TILL THE DAY I DIE
KNOW THIS MUCH IS TRUE
NO MATTER WHAT I DO
OFFEND IN EVERY WAY
SO TELL ME WHAT TO SAY

THE PROTECTOR

JUST NOW
YOU THOUGHT YOU HEARD A SOUND
LOOKING AT THE DOOR
COMING FROM THE FLOOR

I CAN TELL YOU BUT YOU WON'T LISTEN
IVE BEEN WRONG BEFORE MAYBE I'm
WRONG AGAIN
BUT THIS TIME I KNOW ~~BEFORE~~ YOU
HEARD A SOUND BUT

THERES NOONE ELSE AROUND
YOU THOUGHT YOU HEARD A SOUND
~~STILL~~
THE WALLS SPIN AROUND
YOU CAN'T FIGURE IT OUT

I DIDN'T KNOW I WAS A PROTECTOR
BUT I WANT TO DO WHATS CORRECT
NOONE CAN TAKE AWAY MY LIFE
THEY CAN'T ~~TAKE~~ MY ~~MONEY~~ MONEY
OR HURT MY WIFE

Original working lyrics to "This Protector."

1. AND IF IM WASTING MY TIME
THEN NOTHING COULD BE BETTER
THAN STAYING ON THE LINE
AND WAITING FOR AN HONEST
WORD FOREVER.

2. AND IF YOUR SAYING GOODBYE
PLEASE DON'T YOU THINK ME BITTER
FOR RECALLING EVERY RHYME
FROM THE BOOK, THE PAGE, THE LINE,
THE WORD, THE LETTER.

3. THE WINDOWS TURNING BLUE
AND THE WATERS EVER FLOWING
I HOPE IM NOT A FOOL
FOR LAUGHING AT MYSELF
AS YOU WERE GOING.

Handwritten lyrics to "Wasting My Time" (originally titled "Letter.")

① HEY MARY, CAN'T YOU FIND A WAY TO BRING ME DOWN?

② I'M SORRY, THAT ONCE AGAIN I LET YOU DOWN.

③ CHOR) KNOWING YOU IT'S PROBABLY GOING TO BE FINE
BUT THEN AGAIN YOU'LL
PROBABLY CHANGE YOUR MIND

④ SORRY MARY BUT BEING YOUR MATE MEANS TRYING TO DO SOMETHING THAT YOUR NOT GOING TO HATE.

⑤ CHORUS / SOLO

⑥ HEY MARY, CAN'T YOU FIND A WAY TO BRING ME DOWN?

HEY MARY

Original lyrics to "Now Mary" (complete with original title "Hey Mary.")

JUMBLE, JUMBLE

JUMBLE, JUMBLE
ALL AT MY HOUSE
WELL COME ON OVER
SLEEP ON THE COUCH
I CAN'T EVEN SEE YOU
LOOK LIKE A MOUSE

WHATEVER HAPPENED
TO FEEL AT EASE
SO SICK OF WORKING
AND BEGGIN PLEASE
WAIT TILL YOU TRIP AND
THEN BREAK YOUR KNEES

OH THERESA
YOU KNOW I LOVE YOU LIKE A SISTER
KEEP BUSY
KEEP ON WORKING WITH A BUSTER
ILL BE SO PROUD
WELL BE A MADAM AND A MISTER

Original lyrics for "Jumble, Jumble."

RED BOWLING BALL ②
RED BOWLING BALL RUTH

THATS SOMETHING
YOU KNOW THAT ITS THE TRUTH

IM THROWING
ITS GONNA BREAK YOUR TOOTH.

PAY ATTENTION NOW
ATTENTION TO THESE WORDS ①

I LOVE YOU
I DON'T KNOW WHAT YOU HEARD

AND THIS FELLA
HAS. GOT TO GO FOR SURE

HEY FELLA
I THOUGHT I KNOCKED YOU DOWN ③
I LOVE THIS GIRL
SO DON'T YOU COME AROUND

YOU LEAVING
SHOULD BE THE ONLY SOUND

Original handwritten lyrics to "Red Bowling Ball Ruth."

SOMEBODY'S SCREAMING
LOOKING AT THE CEILING

EVERYTHINGS SO FUNNY
I DON'T HAVE ANY MONEY

PEOPLE MAY NOT KNOW ME

BUT THEY KNOW HOW TO SHOW ME

MY PRIDE IS DYING
I THINK I'M ALL DONE LYING

THE ONLY ONE WHO'S SHARING
SO I STOP CARING

ALL ALONE AND WALKING
NOBODY'S TALKING

WIND IS BLOWING
WHERE AM I GOING

OFF A BRIDGE I'M FALLING
NOBODY'S CALLING

ON THE GROUND AND LAYING
NOBODY'S PRAYING

Original lyrics to "Why Can't You Be Nicer to Me?."

ALL THESE PEOPLE
KNOW WHERE THE ACTIONS AT NOW
WALKING DOWN THE STREET
WITH A BASEBALL BAT NOW
ICE CREAM SANDWHICH
AT THE LIQUOR STORE NOW
TAKE YOUR LITTLE SISTER
TO THE RAZOR BALL NOW
LOOKING FOR CHICKS
WITH A CIGARETTE LIGHT
FAMILY PICTURE KNOCKED OVER
IN A TV GAME FIGHT
THATS WHERE THE ACTIONS AT

ALL THESE PEOPLE KNOW
JUST WHAT TO WEAR NOW
THERES A MIRROR IN YOUR FRIENDS
FACE TO COMB YOUR HAIR NOW
YOUR IDOL IS A ROGUE
WHO IS HARD AS HELL NOW
AND YOUR DADDYS GOT A
BACKYARD LAWN TO MOW NOW
PUT A PIECE A PLYWOOD
ON THE BEDROOM DOOR
NEW TENNIS SHOES ON
THE SCHOOL GYM FLOOR

ALL THESE PEOPLE
KNOW EVERYTHING THERE IS
NOW
ASK EM IF THEIR MILK
COMES FROM A COW NOW
FIND THE GAS STATION
ON A MAP OF THE
WORLD NOW
PASS THE ROAD TEST
AT THE AUTO BUREAU NOW
MOTORS NEED OIL
AND THE STOVE NEEDS GAS
BABYS NEED BUTTER
AND MONEY DONT LAST

Working lyrics to "That's Where It's At" which would later evolve into "I Think I Smell a Rat."

① HEY LITTLE APPLE BLOSSOM
WHAT SEEMS TO BE THE PROBLEM
ALL THE ONES YOU TELL YOUR TROUBLES TO
THEY DON'T REALLY CARE FOR YOU

② COME AND TELL ME WHAT YOU'RE THINKING
CAUSE JUST WHEN THE BOAT IS SINKING
A LITTLE LIGHT IS BLINKING
AND I WILL COME AND RESCUE YOU

BRIDGE
LOTS OF GIRLS WALK AROUND IN TEARS
BUT THAT'S NOT FOR YOU
YOU'VE BEEN LOOKING ALL AROUND FOR YEARS
FOR SOMEONE TO TELL YOUR TROUBLES TO

③ COME AND SIT WITH ME AND TALK A WHILE
AND LET ME SEE YOUR PRETTY LITTLE SMILE
PUT YOUR TROUBLES IN A LITTLE PILE
AND I WILL SORT THEM OUT FOR YOU

(SOLO)

BRIDGE

(REPEAT 3)

④

I THINK I'M GONNA MARRY YOU

Handwritten lyrics for "Apple Blossom."

HEY LITTLE APPLE BLOSSOM
WHAT SEEMS TO BE THE PROBLEM
ALL THE PEOPLE THAT
YOU TELL YOUR TROUBLES TO
JUST SEEM TO MAKE IT WORSE
FOR YOU

I LOVE IT WHEN A GIRL LIKE YOU SETTLES FOR A MAN LIKE ME

Unused lyric fragment for "Apple Blossom."

① LOOK ANOTHER WAY GIRL IM TELLIN YA
I GAVE YOU SEVEN MINUTES IN THE MORNING
YOUR MOTHER PUT HER MONEY IN ALUMINUM
NOW YOU'LL NEVER HAVE TO PAY
ATTENTION.

(BONE BROKE)

② LEANIN ON A BRICK WITH MY NAILS
IM TELLIN 'EM THE MONEY'S
IN THE MAIL
KEEP SHOWING THAT MY BONES
NEVER FAKE IT.
NOW THE BRICK BANK IS GONNA BREAK
IT.

(BONE BROKE)

③ LOOK CLOSER YOU CAN SEE HOW I BEEN
RUNNIN IT.
I GOT A DOLLAR BILL IN THE COCKPIT
YOU'RE TURNIN YOURE BACK ON A BLACK HOLE
ILL GET ANOTHER JOB AT THE LIQUOR
STORE.

(BONE BROKE)

KEY OF BBB

Pages 264-265: Working lyrics for "Bone Broke."

① LEANIN ON A BRICK WITH MY NAILS

~~YES~~ ~~BOTTLES~~ ~~APPLES~~

YOU'RE TELLIN ME MONEY'S ~~NEVER FAILS IT~~ IN THE MAIL
NOW I KNOW THAT MY BONES NEVER FAKE IT
NOW ~~A LEAD PIPE IS~~ GONNA BREAK IT
MY EMPTY POCKETS
C.MON
IM BONE BROKE

② LOOK ~~THE~~ ANOTHER WAY GIRL IM TELLIN YA

I GAVE YOU SEVEN MINUTES IN THE MORNING

YOUR MOTHER PUT HER MONEY IN ALUMINUM

NOW YOULL NEVER HAVE TO PAY ATTENTION
NOT ME
IM BONE BROKE

③ LOOK CLOSER YOU CAN SEE HOW I BEEN RUNNIN IT
I GOT ~~AS~~ A DOLLAR BILL IN THE COCKPIT
~~YOU SET IT OFF BETTER WITH A BACK SPIN~~

YOU'RE TURNIN MY BACK ON A BLACK ●HOLE

I'LL GET ANOTHER JOB AT THE LIQUOR STORE

BONE BROKE

IM ~~ALONE~~ AND THE ~~BANK IS GONNA~~
~~BREAK IT~~
KEEP SHOWIN THAT MY BONES NEVER
FAKE IT
NOW THE BRICK BANK IS GONNA
BREAK IT

265

1) HELLO OPERATER — 6
CAN YOU GIVE ME NUMBER 9? — 7
CAN I SEE YOU LATER? — 6
WILL YOU GIVE ME BACK MY DIME? — 7

TURN THE OSCILATER — 6
TWIST IT WITH A DOLLAR BILL — 7
MAILMAN BRING THE PAPER — 6
LEAVE IT ON MY WINDOW SILL — 7

2) FIND A CANARY — 5
BIRD TO BRING MY MESSAGE HOME — 7
CARRY MY OBITUARY — 8
MY A COFFIN DOESN'T HAVE A PHONE — 8
HOW YOU GONNA GET THE MONEY — 8
SEND PAPERS TO AN EMPTY HOME — 8
HOW YOU GONNA GET THE MONEY — 8
NOBODY TO ANSWER THE PHONE? — 8

Original working lyrics for "Hello Operator" complete with counting out of the syllables in each line.

WELL (IM IN A NEW SCHOOL AGAIN)
(WERE BACK IN SCHOOL AGAIN
AND I DON'T REALLY KNOW ANYONE
I REALLY WANNA BE YOUR FRIEND
CAUSE I DON'T REALLY KNOW ANYONE

AND THE BUS IS PULLING
UP TO YOUR HOUSE
I WISH YOU COULD BE SITTING HERE
NEXT TO ME

I DIDN'T SEE U AT SUMMER SCHOOL
BUT I SAW YOU AT THE CORNER STORE
I TRY TO NOT BREAK THE RULES
CAUSE IVE BROKEN THEM ALL BEFORE

BUT EVERY TIME I SEE YOU
I WONDER WHY
I DON'T BREAK A COUPLE RULES
SOA YOU'LL NOTICE ME
TO MAKE YOU 7)

IM STAYIN IN THE BACK OF THE BUS
SO NOBODY WILL NOTICE ME
BUT I HOPE I DON'T STICK OUT TOO MUCH

SISTER DO YOU KNOW MY NAME
IVE THOUGHT ABOUT IT BEFORE AND I WANNA KNOW
SISTER DO YO KNOW MY NAME
I SAID THE SAME THING TO MYSELF JUST A MINUTE AGO

I GOT A FUNNY FEELING
THAT ITS GONNA WORK OUT
CAUSE NOW I SEE YOU
SITTING RIGHT NEXT TO ME — FIN SOFT

SISTER DO YOU KNOW MY NAME

Handwritten lyrics to "Sister, Do You Know My Name?."

(1) IVE THOUGHT ABOUT IT FOR AWHILE
AND IVE THOUGHT ABOUT THE MANY MILES
BUT I THINK ITS TIME THAT IVE GONE AWAY

(2) THE FEELINGS THAT YOU HAVE FOR ME
HAVE GONE AWAY ITS PLAIN TO SEE
AND IT LOOKS TO ME THAT YOU'RE PULLING AWAY

CHORUS

IM GONNA PICK IT UP
IM GONNA PICK IT UP TODAY
IM BOUND TO PACK IT UP
IM BOUND TO PACK IT UP AND GO AWAY
BREAK

(3) I FIND IT HARD TO SAY TO YOU
THAT THIS IS WHAT I HAVE TO DO
BUT THERE IS NO WAY THAT IM GONNA STAY

(4) THERE ARE SO MANY THINGS YOU NEED TO KNOW
AND I WANT TO TELL YOU BEFORE I GO
BUT ITS HARD TO THINK OF JUST WHAT TO SAY

CHORUS

(5) IM SORRY TO LEAVE YOU ALL ALONE
YOURE SITTING SILENT BY THE PHONE
BUT WEVE ALWAYS KNOWN THERE WOULD COME A DAY

(6) THE BUS IS WARM AND SOFTLY LIT
AND A HUNDRED PEOPLE RIDE IN IT
I GUESS IM JUST ANOTHER RUNNING AWAY
CHORUS

Handwritten lyrics for "I'm Bound to Pack It Up."

1) IVE ~~THOUGH~~ THOUGHT ABOUT IT FOR A WHILE
AND I THOUGHT ABOUT THE MANY MILES
BUT I THINK ITS TIME THAT IVE ~~MOVED GONE~~ AWAY

2) THE FEELINGS THAT YOU HAVE FOR ME
HAVE GONE AWAY ITS PLAIN TO SEE
AND IT LOOKS TO ME THAT ~~TODAY THE DAY~~
GT YOURE PULLING AWAY
~~IVE THOUGHT ABOUT YOU EVRY DAY~~
~~I THINK ABOUT IT EVRY DAY~~

3) I FIND IT HARD TO SAY TO YOU
THAT THIS IS WHAT I HAVE TO DO
BUT THERE IS NO WAY THAT IM GONNA STAY

THERE ARE SO MANY THINGS YOU NEED TO KNOW
AND I WANT TO TELL YOU BEFORE I GO
4) BUT ITS HARD TO THINK OF JUST WHAT TO SAY

CHORUS
IM BOUND TO PICK IT UP TODAY
IM BOUND TO PACK IT UP SOMEDAY
AND GO AWAY

5) IM SORRY TO ~~LEAVE~~ LEAVE YOU ALL ALONE
BUT JUST DON'T SIT HOME BY THE PHONE
WEVE ALWAYS KNOWN THAT
YOUVE
YOU'D LEAVE ME TOO IF YOU KNEW A WAY

6) THE BUS IS WARM AND SOFTLY LIT
AND A 100 PEOPLE RIDE IN IT
ONE OF THEM
I GUESS IM JUST ANOTHER PERSON RUNNING AWAY

Working draft of "I'm Bound to Pack it Up."

THE PEN THAT IS INSIDE MY HAND
WRITES DOWN THE WORDS OF EVERY MAN

THE SKIN THAT'S WRAPPED AROUND YOU KNOW

I'M GONNA REACH OUT AND PEEL IT AWAY

I'M GONNA CATCH YOU NOW
(1
AND SING YOU AWAY

Pages 270-271: Unused lyric fragment for "I'm Bound to Pack it Up."

① YOUR SISTERS CLEARLY OUT OF LUCK
AND ALL THE BOARDS THAT HOLD YOU UP
ALL THE NEIGHBORS SAY
YOU GOTTA PUT IT AWAY

② ~~TO~~ TO DO WHAT YOU WANT BUT ~~BE~~ BE POLITE
WHEN THE PEOPLE NEXT DOOR PUT UP A FIGHT

IM BOUND TO PACK IT UP
IM BOUND TO PACK IT UP
AND MOVE AWAY
MAYBE IF I'M GOOD ENOUGH
I CAN STAY

③

DON'T TELL ME THAT YOU HAVE A HEART

IM GONNA
PACK IT UP

1) GOT A LITTLE BIRD
GONNA TAKE HER HOME
PUT HER IN A CAGE
DISCONNECT THE PHONE

2) WHEN I GET YA HOME
THIS IS HOW IT GOES
~~XXXXXXXXX~~ I GOT NOTHIN TO LOSE
ILL NEVER LET YOU GO

3) IF YA GIMME A LOOK
IM GONNA GET THE BOOK
IM GONNA PREACH THE WORD
I WANNA PREACH TO BIRDS
AS I WALK THE FLOOR
YEAH THIS I KNOW

Pages 272-273: Handwritten lyrics for "Little Bird."

GOT A LITTLE BIRD
GONNA TAKE HER HOME
PUT HER IN A CAGE
~~NEVER LEAVE HER ALONE~~
IM GONNA PET YOUR FEATHERS
DISCONNECT THE PHONE GIRL

WHEN I GET YA HOME
~~GONNA SEE YOUR DAD~~
~~TELL EM I LOVE THE BIRD~~
AND THAT IM ALL YOU HAVE

IM GONNA GET THE BOOK
IM GONNA ~~THE~~ PREACH THE WORD
I WANNA PREACH TO BIRDS
AS I WALK THE FLOOR
YEAH THIS I KNOW

1) OH YEAH YOU'RE PRETTY GOOD LOOKING
   FOR A GIRL
   BUT YOUR BACK IS SO BROKEN
   AND THIS FEELING'S STILL GONNA
   LINGER ON
   UNTIL THE YEAR 2525 NOW

2) YEAH YOU'RE PRETTY GOOD LOOKING
   FOR A GIRL
   YOUR EYES ARE WIDE OPEN
   AND YOUR THOUGHTS HAVE BEEN STOLEN
   BY THE BOYS
   WHO TOOK YOU OUT AND BOUGHT YOU EVERYTHING YOU WANT NOW

3) YEAH YOU'RE PRETTY GOOD LOOKING
   OH YEAH

   FOR A GIRL

CHORUS
   LOTS OF PEOPLE IN THIS WORLD
   BUT I WANNA BE YOUR BOY
   I KNOW THAT THOUGHT IS SOUNDING SO ABSURD
   AND I DON'T WANNA BE YOUR TOY

4) JUST CAUSE YOUR PRETTY GOOD LOOKING
   FOR A GIRL
   MY FUTURE'S WIDE OPEN
   BUT THIS FEELINGS STILL GONNA
   BE AROUND
   UNTIL I KNOW EVERYTHING I NEED TO KNOW NOW

5) YEAH YOU'RE PRETTY GOOD LOOKING OH YEAH

Handwritten lyrics to "You're Pretty Good Looking (for a Girl)."

MY BABY'S GOT A HOME OF STONE
CAN'T YOU PEOPLE JUST LEAVE HER ALONE
SHE NEVER DID NOTHIN TO HURT YOU
SO JUST LEAVE HER ALONE

THE MOTION OF HER TINY HANDS
AND THE QUIVER OF HER BONES BELOW
ARE THE ~~tell tale~~ SIGNS OF A GIRL ALONE
AND TELL YOU EVERYTHING YOU NEED TO KNOW

I CAN'T EXPLAIN IT
I FELT IT OFTEN
EVERYTIME I SEE HER FACE
BUT THE WAY ~~YOU TREAT~~ YOU TREAT HER
FILLS ME WITH RAGE
MAKES ME WANT TO TEARAPART THIS PLACE

YOU ~~_~~ TELL ~~_~~ TRY TO TELL HER WHAT TO DO
AND ALL SHE DOES IS STARE AT YOU
HER STARE IS LOUDER THAN YOUR VOICE
TRUTH DOESN'T MAKE A NOISE

Handwritten lyrics to "Truth Doesn't Make a Noise."

ASTRO

MAYBE MOM CAN DO THE ASTRO?
MAYBE MOM CAN DO THE ASTRO?
MAYBE MOM CAN DO THE ASTRO, ASTRO

MAYBE DAD CAN DO THE ASTRO?

MAYBE MEG CAN DO THE ASTRO
MAYBE JACK CAN DO THE ASTRO

MAYBE ORSON DOES THE ASTRO
MAYBE TESLA DOES THE ASTRO

MAYBE EDISON IS AC DC

MAYBE ELRO DOES THE ASTRO
MAYBE JASPER DOES THE ASTRO

WE DONT KNOW

WE DONT KNOW

Working lyrics for "Astro."

MARANTETTE
LEVERETTE
LANNETTE
LA FAYETTE
LIVERNOIS

ROUGE

LE BLANC

ROCHELLE
MARCELLE
RIOPELLE
MANISTIQUE
N ARMOUR

LA BROSSE

LA BROSSE

MERCIER
LE MAY
TOURNIER
SALLIOTE
N LE ROY

LOUIS

LOUIS

MONTLIEU
CADIEUX
NEVEUX
AVENUE
EN DETROIT

I'M
READY
TO ROCK
N ROLL

Working lyrics for "Lafayette Blues."

277

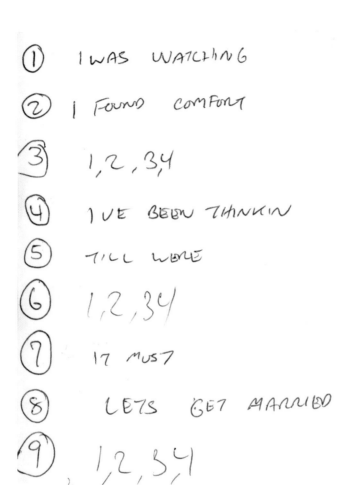

1. I WAS WATCHING
2. I FOUND COMFORT
3. 1, 2, 3, 4
4. IVE BEEN THINKIN
5. TILL WERE
6. 1, 2, 3, 4
7. IT MUST
8. LETS GET MARRIED
9. 1, 2, 3, 4

"HOTEL YORBA"

Pages 278-280: Working lyrics for "Hotel Yorba."

IVE FOUND COMFORT
IN SOME THOUGHTS TURNIN
  WHEELS AROUND
I SAID 39 TIMES THAT I LOVE U
TO THE BEUTY I HAD FOUND

IVE BEEN THINKIN
OF A LITTLE PLACE DOWN BY THE LAKE
THEY GOT A DIRTY OLD ROAD
LEADIN UP TO THE HOUSE I WONDER HOW
  LONG IT WILL TAKE

TILL WERE ALONE
SITTIN ON THE FRONT PORCH OF THAT
  ~~HOUSE~~ HOME
STOMPIN OUR FEET ON THE WOODEN FLOOR

IT MUST SOUND SILLY
FOR ME TO THINK CHILDISH THOUGHTS
LIKE THESE
BUT IM SO TIRED OF ACTING HARD TOUGH
NOW IM GONNA DO WHAT I PLEASE

"HOTEL YORBA"

WELL IT LOOKS LIKE RAIN
BETTER GRAB YOUR UMBRELLA

TRY TO DO YOUR BEST TO FILL
THIS VACANCY

3 WALLS AND OPEN AIR
YOURE FORCING ME TO STARE
AT THE FLOOR AND OUT THE DOOR
IN THE DRAWER

WELL THE EARTH IS DIRTY
EVERYONE LOOKS THE OTHER WAY
SOMETIMES I THINK THERE AINT MUCH TO DO
AND A WHOLE LOT LESS TO SAY

THEN I START THINKING

"HOTEL YORBA"

why cant you be nicer to me

1.   somebodys screaming
looking at the ceiling
oh oh
everythings so funny
i dont have any money
oh oh
people dont even know me
but i bet they know how to show me
oh oh

2.   my pride is dying
i think im all done lying
oh oh
nobodys sharing
so i stop caring
oh oh
all alone and walking
nobodys talking
oh oh

3.   well the wind is blowing
where am i going
oh oh
off a bridge and falling
nobodys calling
oh oh
on the ground and laying
nobodys praying
oh oh

Pages 282-289: Typewritten lyrics intended for insert to self-titled album.

SUZY LEE

1. theres a story
   i would like to tell
   my problem is
   its one you know to well

2. miss suzy lee
   the one im thinking of
   the question is
   is she the one i love

3. she sent me flowers
   with tears burned inside
   do you know what id do?
   i would run an hide
   i would run and hide

4. and a paper
   on it was my name
   with the question
   do you feel the same?
   do you feel the same?

5. to end this tale
   the one im speaking of
   i wish i had an answer but i just dont know
   is this really love
   is this really love

dead leaves and the dirty ground
when i know your not around
1. shiny tops and soda pops
when i hear your lips make a sound

30 notes in the mailbox
will tell you that im coming home
2. and i think im gonna stick around
for a while so youre not alone
for a while so youre not alone

if you can hear a piano fall
you can hear me coming down the hall
3. if i could just hear your pretty voice
i dont think i need to see at all
i dont think i need to see at all

soft hair and a velvet tongue
i wanna give you what you give to me
4. every breath that is in your lungs
is a tiny little gift to me

well the man with the microphone
can tell you what he loves the most
5. and you know why you love at all
if youre thinking of the holy ghost

JIMMY THE EXPLODER

1. NOW JIMMY DO YOU WANT AN EXPLOSION NOW
   NOW JIMMY DO YOU WANT TO EXPLODE NOW

2. YEAH MONKEY ARE YOU SEEING RED NOW
   YEAH MONKEY JUMPING ON THE BED NOW

   HOO   HOO   HJOO HOO   HOO   HOO

3. GREEN APPLES ON THE TREE AND GROWING NOW
   GREEN APPLES ARE GONNA BE EXPLODING NOW

LETS BUILD A HOME

1. some bricks now baby
   lets build a home
   some bricks now baby
   lets build a home cmon

2. im getting lazy
   throw me a bone
   im getting lazy
   throw me a bone cmon

RED BOWLING BALL RUTH

1. well pay attention
   attention to my words
   i love you
   i dont know what you heard
   and this fellow has got to go for sure

2. red bowling ball
   red bowling ball ruth
   thats something
   that makes you know the truth
   i set it rolling
   and then it breaks your tooth

3. well peter
   i think youre in the wrong town
   i love this girl
   so dont you come around
   and you leaving will be the only sound

LITTLE PEOPLE

1. theres a little girl who says
    bing bing bop
    theres a little girl who says
    bing bing bop
    hello
    oh oh

2. theres a little boy with a
    spider in his hand

3. theres a little girl wwith
    the red shoes on

4. theres a little boy with
    25 cents

5. theres a little girl with
    a tiger on her bed

6. theres a little boy with
    nothing on his mind

BROKEN BRICKS

1. have you been to the broken bricks gt
   girl
     snuck down thru the cyclone fence
past the caution tape
the security gate backwords to the
breakroom bench

theres a little corner where you first
got kissed felt her boyfriends fist
and made the company list
and theres a little spot where your dad
ate lunch and your brother landed
his first punch

2/ have you been to the brocken bricks girl
seen the barrels that they left behind
seen the machine that cut aluminum clean
duct tape on a caution sign
broken tooth window panes
drip a rusty colored rain
to drive a man insane
you try to jump the water but you land in oil
cliumb the metal of a broken crane

3. dont go to the broken bricks girl
its not the place that you want to be
think about the spot
your father spent his life
demolition calls it building "c"

Original working draft lyrics for "Hand Springs."

SOMEBODY WALKED UP TO ME BUT I DIDN'T KNOW
WHAT TO DO

SOMEBODY SAID HELLO TO ME BUT I DIDN'T
KNOW WHAT TO DO

AND NOW I THINK THAT MY WORDS COULD
GET TWISTED SO I BOWD MY BACK
OVER TAKE A GULP BE FUNNY
CAUSE I KNOW THERES NOTHIN ELSE
TO DO.

MY MOTION TRIED TO PICK ME UP
WHEN I WAS SITTING DOWN ON THE GROUND

SOMETHING FORCED MY LITTLE EYES
TO OPEN BUT I COULDN'T MAKE OUT THE SOUND

NOW I THINK THAT MY EYES ARE
LYING ~~THAT THEY~~ AND THEY DON'T HAVE EMOTION
DON'T WANNA BE SOCIAL GOTTA GO
COUNT MILLIN CAUSE THERES
NOTHIN ELSE I CAN DO

Working lyrics for "Do."

YOU'VE GOT HER IN YOUR POCKET
AND THERE'S NO WAY OUT NOW
PUT HER IN THE SAFE AND LOCK IT
CAUSE ITS HOME SWEET HOME

NOBODY EVER LET U KNOW THAT
ITS THE WRONG WAY
THINK ITS FUNNY THAT THE FIRST
YOU MET WAS ON A SUNDAY
IF SHE SICKS AROUND THEN YOU MUST
BE ALRIGHT
BUT THINGS ARE COMING TO HER WHEN
YOU'RE OUT OF SIGHT — AT NIGHT

Original handwritten draft for "You've Got Her in Your Pocket."

Meg White's original handwritten ideas for the lyrics to "Little People."

ALL ALONE AND WALKING
NOBODYS TALKING
OH

ITS NOT HAPPENING WITH MY FINGERS
THE BACK ROW OF THE CHOIR SINGERS
OH

I GOT A BASEBALL DUSTY
I GUESS I MUST BE RUSTY
OH

THE CORNER OF A DIAMOND STONE
IS SHARPER THAN A FINGER BONE
OH

WHEN YOU LIKE EVERYBODY
BUT EVERYBODY DON'T LIKE YOU
OH

RED ROSES CUTTING
YOUR OWN HEART LEFT BEHIND

15 YEARS ~~EATER~~ AFTER
THERE WILL BE LAUGHTER
OH
THE OTHERS

Pages 294-295: Assorted unused lyrics for "Why Can't You be Nicer to Me?."

SOMEBODYS SCREAMING
NO BODYS ORGASMING
WITHIN A MIRROR
IS THIS PERFECT SINNER
NOWHERE BUT NOWHERE
AND NOT ONE THING TO SHARE
– OH OH OH
LIKE A PUPPY FOLLOWS
EVERY MOTION HOLLOW
COME BACK COME BACK
FIND BEUTY IN SOMETHING
BEFORE YOU CANT FIND NOTHING
TALKING SMOKY HALF SLANG
SHOULD BE COMING UP WITH A WHIRBANG
PEPPERMINT AND GLASSES
WE KNOW HOW COOL THAT IS
~~WORKING ON~~
CANT BE WORKING ON NOTHIN
TO BUSY DOIN' NOTHIN'
OH

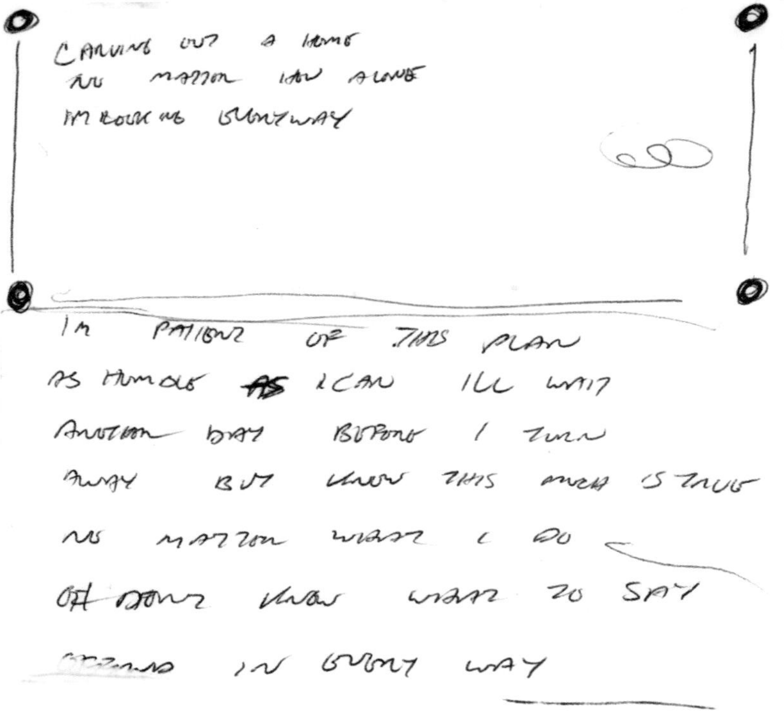

CARVING OUT A HOME
NO MATTER HOW ALONE
I'M LOOKING EVERYWAY

I'M PATIENT OF THIS PLAN
AS HUMBLE ~~AS~~ I CAN I'LL WAIT
ANOTHER DAY BEFORE I TURN
AWAY BUT KNOW THIS MUCH IS TRUE
NO MATTER WHAT I DO
OH DON'T KNOW WHAT TO SAY
OFFEND IN EVERY WAY

Lyric fragment for "Offend in Every Way."

1) WHAT'S THAT SHE SAID?
WHAT'S THAT SHE SAID WITH HER
FINGERS TURNIN BLUE (WHITE)
AND HER FACE WAS TURNIN RED

2) WAS THAT YOUR DAD?
WAS THAT YOUR DAD
WITH THE MAGIC MARKER WRITING
LITTLE ANGEL ON YOUR HEAD

3) I THINK YOU'RE DEAD
I THINK YOU'RE DEAD
CAUSE YOU NEVER SAY NOTHING
WHEN YOU'RE LYING ON THE BED

Handwritten lyrics for "Red Death at 6:14."

NOBODY EVER TOLD YOU THAT IT WAS
THE WRONG WAY

I MUST BE FUNNY TO T

DON'T YOU KNOW THAT EVERY THING HAS
TO END SOMEDAY

BUT NOT THIS TIME YOU SAY
YOU'RE DOING IT RIGHT

CAUSE YOU KNOW THAT SHE'S NOT
GONNA PUT UP A FIGHT

NOT TONIGHT SO

SOMETIMES I WONDERED HOW MUCH
I'M SUPPOSED TO PAY ATTENTION
SHOW

I CAN'T EXACTLY WALK RIGHT BY
WITHOUT A MENTION

WHEN I THINK ABOUT IT
I CAN'T LOOK AWAY

AT OTHER TIMES I THINK,
KNOW
JUST WHAT TO SAY
NOT WORRY

Pages 298-299: Working lyrics for "You've Got Her in Your Pocket."

YOUVE GOT HER IN YOUR POCKET
AND THERES NO WAY OUT NOW
PUT HER IN THE SAFE AND LOCK IT
CAUSE ITS HOME SWEET HOME

AINT IT NICE WHEN YOU DONT HAVE TO FIGHT FOR
YOUR

IT SOMETIMES TAKES A WHILE WHEN

ITS DIFFICULT TO FIGURE OUT
WHEN I WISH THAT THE RIGHT IDEA
TO YOU WITHOUT A DOUBT

PEOPLES OPINION ABOUT WHAT YOU
ARE SUPPOSED TO DO
NOW TRADITION COULD BE
BAD IF YOU ONLY KNOW
SHOWS YOU BE HAPPY THAT
YOU HAVE SOMBODY AND
SHELL NEVER GO

YOU TRICKED HER JUST ENOUGH
FORCE HER TO FALL IN LOVE
YOU AINT FIGHT SOTHING TIGHT

THE BIG 3 KILLED MY BABY.

THEY DOWNSIZE THE EASY WAY
TO DECREASE THE PAY DAY
IM NOT BIG ENOUGH TO CHANGE YOURE PLAY
LOOKOUT EL NIÑOS COMIN YOURE WAY

THE BIG 3 KILLED MY BABY
NOBODYS COMIN HOME AGAIN

30,000 WHEELS ARE ROLLIN
AND MY STICK SHIFT HANDS ARE SWOLLEN
ALL THESE PEOPLE STUCK IN THE MUD
THE MOTORS RUNNIN ON TUCKERS BLOOD
EVERYTHING INVOLVED IS SHADY
THE BIG 3 KILLED MY BABY

DON'T LET EM TELL YOU THE FUTURES ELEC TRIC
THE GASOLINES NOT MEASURED IN METRIC
30,000 WHEELS ARE SPINNIN
JIMMY DODGES FACE IS GRINNIN'
NOW MY HANDS ARE TURNIN RED
THEN I FIND OUT MY BABYS DEAD

Pages 300-301: Handwritten lyrics to "The Big Three Killed My Baby."

THE BIG 3 KILLED MY BABY
- 30,000 WHEELS ARE ROLLIN .
AND MY STICK SHIFT HANDS
ARE SWOLLEN
- EVERYTHING INVOLVED IS SHADY
THE BIG 3

TOOK AWAY TH

THEY DOWNSIZE THE EASY WAY
TO DECREASE THE PAY DAY
/ C

I'M ~~NOT~~ BIG ENOUGH TO CHANGE
YOURE PLAY
LOOKOUT EL NINOS COMIN YOURE WAY

THEY DOWNSIZE THE EASY WAY
TO DECREASE THE PAY DAY
I'M NOT BIG ENOUGH
TO CHANGE YOUR PLAY
LOOKOUT EL NINO'S COMIN YOUR WAY

THE BIG 3 [CHORUS]
KILLED MY BABY
NOBODY'S COMIN
HOME AGAIN

Original intro lyrics for "The Big Three Killed My Baby" written specifically large so that Andre Williams could read them.

PHOTO CREDITS

pg. 26, Ko Melina Zydeco
pgs. 40-41, Ko Melina Zydeco
pgs. 70-71, Ben Blackwell
pg. 84, Patrick Pantano
pg. 96, John Baker
pg. 116, Patrick Pantano
pgs. 146-147, Ewen Spencer
pgs. 168-169, Patrick Keeler
pgs. 194-195, David James Swanson
pg. 212, Patrick Pantano
pgs. 222-223, Patrick Pantano
pg. 243, Patrick Pantano
pgs. 246-247, Patrick Pantano
pg. 260, Patrick Pantano
pg. 281, Patrick Pantano
pg. 303, Patrick Pantano